Stain the Water Clear

Merry Christmas
Lala

Love Barbara

Dec. 25, 2003

Stain the Water Clear

❖

A Collection of Rural Pen and Yankee Doodlin' Columns, 1993-2002

by Luanne Austin

Writer's Showcase
New York Lincoln Shanghai

Stain the Water Clear

A Collection of Rural Pen and Yankee Doodlin' Columns, 1993-2002

Writer's Showcase
an imprint of iUniverse, Inc.

For information address:
iUniverse, Inc.
2021 Pine Lake Road, Suite 100
Lincoln, NE 68512
www.iuniverse.com

ISBN: 0-595-25802-6 (pbk)
ISBN: 0-595-65347-2 (cloth)

Printed in the United States of America

To Kim, Heidi, Daniel and Rachel

"Piper sit thee down and write
In a book that all may read"—
So he vanish'd from my sight.
And I pluck'd a hollow reed,

And I made a rural pen,
And I stain'd the water clear,
And I wrote my happy songs
Every child may joy to hear.
—from "Songs of Innocence" by William Blake

Contents

Acknowledgements

Thanks to my first editors, Joe Fitzgerald and Joe Emerson, for taking a chance and putting their faith in my abilities. Thanks to my readers for all the affirming letters, faxes e-mails, telephone calls and personal visits over the years. Thanks to my family for letting me use you as column material. Thanks so much to Kim, for believing in the best of me.

Thanks also to Donovan Douglas for his lovely work on the book cover.

Introduction

I began writing columns for the Daily News-Record while stringing for the newspaper in 1993. The every-other-weekly column was called "Southern Yankee," about life in the South as a transplanted New Yorker. I was amazed at the volume of letters I received in response to those columns.

Some came from other transplants.

"...It is comforting to know that someone else is going through what I had gone through. The adjustment period was hard and it took longer to get used to this area than I had anticipated.... To break away is hard but in the long run you become stronger and wiser." (Laurie.C., Broadway, Va.)

When I joined the staff at the newspaper later that year, the managing editor informed me they would no longer pay me to write columns. I was free to continue, though, if I wanted to. I declined. Within a few months, the editor had received so much flack for discontinuing my column, he asked me to start writing them again, for pay.

When I returned, I renamed the column "Yankee Doodlin'," which I felt would alert my old readers while freeing me to write on a broader range of topics. I'd exhausted the north/south issues and was ready to move on to other things: family life, faith, American culture and anything else that happened to capture my thoughts. The letters kept coming.

After a few years, the "Yankee" felt outdated. I chose another name—one that I'd been mulling over since the previous renaming—that more accurately represented what I'd grown into as a writer. Rural Pen.

"And with my rural pen I stained the water clear..."

That line in a song by Terry Scott Taylor had taken me on a search for its origin. Taylor wrote more than one song while under the influence of the 18th century poet, William Blake, and the words intrigued me.

Finding the poem was not easy. I had little poetry in my house. In a second-hand bookshop downtown, I purchased a copy of *The Norton Anthology of English Literature*. In it, I found in Blake's introduction to *Songs of Innocence* these words:

"And I made a rural pen and I stain'd the water clear..."

I read more. Then moved on to *Songs of Experience*.

"Tyger! Tyger! burning bright
In the forests of the night,
What immortal hand or eye
Could frame thy fearful symmetry?"

Reading Blake's poetry felt like an act of rebellion. But I kept reading because his words touched something deep inside me, expressed something in me I did not know was there.

The more I read, the more I wanted. As I read Blake's poetry, and then that of others—Christina Rossetti, T.S. Eliot, Robert Browning—something gave birth in me, an other self. Or perhaps it was a dormant self come to life. You see, for years I had read nothing outside the parameters set by the group with which I identified myself. Not that it was forbidden. There was no power to do that. It was more understood: We read these authors, listen to these speakers, go to these seminars, think this way about these issues.

All well and OK, but...I suppose most of us human beings need to identify ourselves with a group that has a purpose, but...when it confines us, stifles us, prevents us from searching, thinking, growing and learning, it ceases to be beneficial.

This is true of jobs, relationships, religions, clubs, hobbies, sports. When everything and everyone we read and watch and listen to and associate with are all of the same ilk, we cease to be able to see clearly. Our brains, already operating at a finite capacity, shrink ever more.

I felt like I'd been eating nothing but broccoli and carrots for a long time and suddenly had been introduced to the taste of chicken, and then potatoes, and apples and rice. Once I had tasted other foods and became healthier, I could not go back to a restrictive diet.

I'm certainly not saying that now I am the enlightened one. Far from it. Every time a curtain parts to show me another aspect of truth, it makes me realize how little I know. As a writer, understanding comes as I see my words form on the page. From my scribbling rural pen emerges clarity.

> *"If you get simple beauty and naught else,*
> *You get about the best thing God invents:*
> *That's somewhat: and you'll find the soul you have missed,*
> *Within yourself, when you return him thanks."*
>
> —Robert Browning

Over the years, many folks have asked for a book of my columns. While I was always flattered by this request, I did not want to end up with 1,000 books under my bed, pitifully peddling them at every public event I attended. So I procrastinated.

Finally, it was time. Past time.

This collection begins with some of my earliest columns, and includes a variety of topics from over the years. The chapters are divided into subjects. I picked my favorites, which have not always been those of my readers. If I've missed any, please let me know. Perhaps they can be included in another volume.

Yankee Doodlin'

○ ○

"Now the Lord said to Abram, 'Go from your country and your kindred and your father's house to the land that I will show you."

—Genesis 12:1

Happy Being South Bound

As a young New York City suburb-bred woman, moving to the Shenandoah Valley was the realization of my longings. My husband and I had planned and saved for months, sold most of our earthly possessions and packed what was left on a flatbed truck covered with a canvas tarp.

During the months of our preparation, seasoned travelers offered much advice about what to expect living in Virginia. A retired judge informed me of the backward ways of Virginians—how incest was still rampant, that they still used outhouses and that I would end up barefoot and toothless, saddled with 14 kids.

My mother announced that I would never survive the "sultry" weather. People told my husband he'd never make more than $100 per week. And I was doomed to getting fat on fried chicken, lard-soaked grits and black-eyed peas.

In spite of all the kindly warnings, we left Long Island at midnight, Sept. 14, 1978. Our two children, ages 3 and six months, were squeezed into the truck's cab with us and a few cartons of leftover chow mein (the last good Chinese food we'd eat for years).

The truck looked like a Conestoga wagon and it drove like one, too. When, 16 hours later, we took a shortcut from I-81 over the Massanutten Mountain to the town of Shenandoah (I didn't see the mountain on the map), our soon-to-die engine could have used a few more horses. As it was, we forged our way over in first gear at five mph.

At the top, a glorious site welcomed us to Page Valley. The rolling patchwork quilt of green pastures, bronzed cornfields and golden grasses looked like a storybook picture. It was home as soon as I saw it.

Our first taste of Southern hospitality came the next day, when our new neighbors in the apartment building helped us unpack our truck. Afterward they said, "Y'all come see us, now."

Our first experience with local radio came Monday morning when, instead of hearing about the weekend murders and robberies, and how far the traffic was backed up on the Long Island Expressway, we heard

Homer reporting on hog prices and people's birthdays and telling corny jokes. We sat on the floor of our furnitureless apartment and laughed and laughed.

Over the next few months, we discovered many differences in northern and southern ways of living. Like being called "ma'am" and having to wait in the checkout line while the cashier listened to a detailed description of her third cousin's hysterectomy. Stuff like that drove me crazy.

But we like it here. In the hollow where we now live, when the lights go out on a moonless night, it is black. The silence used to keep me awake—I was accustomed to the sound of police sirens, train whistles and screeching tires. Now the only sound is the lullaby of Naked Creek splashing its way to the Shenandoah River.

It's home.

Living Off the Land

To consumers in the midst of American Dream suburbia, the Shenandoah Valley seemed like the perfect place to fulfill our youthful dream of "living off the land."

My husband and I spent hours poring over Mother Earth News and Organic Gardening magazines. I imagined myself milking the cow, churning butter, baking bread in a woodstove, canning apples and peaches from the orchard. Buying acreage on Long Island was not an option.

We wanted to live *off* the land, not *for* the land. For example, my mother-in-law just sold her seven-room house on a small development lot for $160,000. Maybe that's not so bad. But her taxes, had she stayed there, would have been $5,400 this year. Tack the average $600–$1200 mortgage payment onto that and see what you come up with.

Our home here in the hollow cost $20,000 (it did need some work) for seven acres of woods and pasture, with an everlasting spring and stream. Since buying the adjacent four acres with barn, our taxes are just under $300 a year.

We nurtured 25 baby chicks (via the Sears catalog) with a light bulb in a child's pool. Soon we had three cows (I think two were bulls), three pigs, three goats, a dog and cat. We had the upper garden and the lower garden. We had the compost heap. We collected the eggs, milked the goats, and slopped the hogs.

When my father (a Connecticut businessman) came to visit he said, "Luanne, I've wanted to do a lot of things in my life, but this was never one of them."

Besides the relatives' incredulity, we had one major problem—no fence. Well, I guess it was a fence at one time, but it sure didn't keep the animals in. Once a neighbor called to say that when she'd opened her front door, my goat (Olivia) had bolted into the house and leapt onto her couch. Sometimes we didn't know where the heck the animals had wandered off to, and spent hours combing the mountains for them. The hollow folks must've watched us ignorant Yankees with a chuckle.

And the garden. Being organically inclined, we wouldn't spray with chemicals, so rabbits and bugs devoured much of our "crop." Squishing beetles with my fingers got old fast.

The soil was different too. Long Island earth had few rocks but a lot of sand in it, making it naturally loamy (they say the Island is a topsoil-and-sand deposit of the Ice Age). The red clay here and rocks, rocks, rocks were a challenge to deal with. My husband put an engine on the archaic David Bradley plow we found on the property, but I think shoveling would have been easier.

And I never knew that string beans actually had strings on them. I just followed the cookbook's freezing directions and stuck 'em in the freezer. That night I cooked fresh ones and what a surprise. My first venture into food preservation ended up in the compost heap.

Now the chickens and pigs and goats are gone. We have horses and cows grazing in a (fenced) pasture. We never did plant he orchard, but do tend a small garden. I don't can anything.

And when the mood strikes, I bake bread in the gas oven and scarf them down with (store-bought) butter.

From Streetwise to Countrywise

To the novice, making one's way down a New York City sidewalk can be a scary ordeal. Here's what I saw, heard and smelled on a trek from Penn Station at 34th St. to Lincoln Center at 65th St.:

Rich old debutantes, flaunting the latest Christian Dior, walking Lhasa Aphsos and Great Danes on jeweled leashes; busy executives dashing, portfolios under arm, to important meetings; haggard bag ladies and smelly drunks dozing fitfully on warm subway grates; long haired hippies peddling drugs at curbside, broadcasting their wares to passersby; scantily-clad unsmiling prostitutes, from ages 11 to 65, strutting and strolling the pavement; a dementoid shouting, "Nothing is real, it's all an illusion!"; panhandlers pleading for quarters for "a cup of coffee, man."

How does one make his way through this gushing, somewhat dangerous, stream of humanity?

My mother, a secretary at United Artists in her younger days, taught me how: keep a brisk pace, posture erect, eyes straight ahead. Nobody bothers you.

I may have been street-wise, but I definitely was not countrywise when I moved to this hollow. Moving to the country was such a euphoric contemplation—I didn't realize the fears that lay within. Well-meaning friends warned me about snakes—creatures I'd seen only in movies and at the Bronx Zoo. Now I envisioned them slithering towards me from every direction. So I used some logic based on the old premise that "they're more afraid of you than you are of them." OK. I assumed that snakes have ears (do they?). My tactic, in walking across a grassy field, was to sing loudly—usually a per-version of "The Happy Wanderer".

"I am a happy wanderer, as happy as can be,
And if by chance I see a snake,
from me he'll have to flee,

Val-der-ee, val-der-a, val-der-a,
Val-der-a-ha-ha-ha-ha-ha…"

Sometimes I would talk loudly to the imaginary snakes—"Okay, Mr. Snake, here I come. You'd better get outta my way. Here I come…"

I never did see any snakes, just a worm every now and then.

Then we had this great idea to raise calves bought at a dairy farm. I saw myself rising early, skipping to the barn and serenely nursing a cute little calf. But they were strong little boogers. They pushed me around and jerked the bottle out of my hand. At first, I dropped the bottle on the ground and ran for safety. But the monsters had to be fed or they'd starve and we'd be out a hundred bucks. So I held my body away from them, at like a 45-degree angle, and cried the whole time they were feeding.

And I didn't know what was lurking in the woods. Bears, raccoons, possum, deer, chipmunks, skunks, mountain lions, wildebeest—all, in my imagination at least, waiting to tear me to pieces with every step. I felt like Dorothy walking down the yellow brick road: "Lions and tigers and bears, oh, my!"

The most dangerous critters I came across were red squirrels.

My worst fear was of the hounds and beagles that stood in the way of my daily run. The guy across the street must've had 20,000 hunting dogs roaming around. After a few clashes with them chasing and barking and howling at me, I stopped running. For months.

Finally, though, I became determined to run, and to hell with the dogs. A deep instinct rose to my consciousness: keep a brisk pace, posture erect, eyes straight ahead.

The dogs never bothered me.

Moving Away from Mom and Dad

Living away from family brings up issues all "transplanted" people deal with. Those from close families grapple with their decision to move away. Some, whose families are not so close, are apathetic about leaving. Others are glad to escape family problems or interference.

In 1978, at age 24, I was excited about the adventure of launching my new life in Virginia. I felt little remorse at moving 500 miles away from my family. They had always kept their proper distance while remaining within reach.

So I was surprised at how I missed them after we moved. Gazing north out my apartment window, crying, I wondered if they'd ever come see me. On my birthday I moped around, imagining they'd all forgotten me. Late that afternoon, a UPS man delivered a package—a copper teapot with porcelain handle and gourmet teas from my dad. He remembered!

Holidays were hard too, but we've since devised our own customs. Our Thanksgiving tradition is to never spend it the same way twice. That first year we invited a poor man with no family to dinner. Sometimes we've had other transplanted families over, gone to New York, or had relatives visit us. One year we butchered hogs all day with the Kline clan. The last time I saw my dad healthy was the Thanksgiving he spent with us.

When we visited him in Connecticut the day after Christmas, he was dying. We'd been looking forward to a celebration because my sister from Ireland was there with her family. But Dad was always the one who made holidays fun and he was ill from a stroke. He went to the hospital the morning we left. I felt uneasy leaving him.

He was in and out of the hospital for two months after that, suffering stroke after stroke. I knew going up there with my kids would be too burdensome for everyone. If I went alone, what would I do with the kids? And do I really want to see him in this condition?

When my stepmother called to say the doctor was taking him off life support, my husband and children left with me immediately. Dad died an hour before our arrival.

This is the hardest part of living away from family. After both my parents' deaths I was able to spend only a few days with my brother and sisters—crying, remembering, laughing, holding each other.

There's no way to keep up with the day-to-day of your family's lives unless you're into $100+phone bills. You learn to make decisions, accomplish goals and get through life without their support or, conversely, without being hindered by their disapproval. In short, you grow up.

I see in many families who live close together (or have $100-plus phone bills) too much dependence on Mama or Daddy or siblings. They often have difficulty forming close relationships outside the family, haven't the benefit of other viewpoints in making decisions, and spouses carry resentment of in-law's interference. Often, differing from the family's lifestyle brings such sharp criticism that they either live with strife or conform to the family's way of life.

If I had my druthers, all my relatives would move to Washington, D.C. I'd see them more often, but not too much.

Because I do still miss them sometimes.

The Holler Party

After living in these mountains for twelve years, I was invited to a party in the hollow. Maybe that gives you an idea of how long it takes to gain acceptance back here.

I was a bit nervous. Party noises—loud country music, drunken laughter, cars peeling out, yelling and shooting—have drifted into my open windows on many a warm summer night. Rumors of fights and jealous husbands sometimes circulate for weeks afterwards.

When I arrived at this party, I was greeted by a rattlesnake writhing on the ground near the back deck. Folks were gathered around watching it. This aroused my suspicions, because I know most holler people (most sane people) have a deathly fear of snakes of any type. As it turned out, the viper had been beheaded hours before, a fact it didn't seem to be aware of. It coiled several times and tried to strike at what it couldn't see. The nerves and muscles that move its strong jaw were futilely snapping at the air.

The snake provided the party with entertainment for hours, and, I must admit, it was entertaining. Watching it inspired the men to tell tales about the biggest, baddest snakes they'd ever killed. Whenever the snake became still someone would go over and kick it around to get it moving again. One man said that its nerve center was in its tail and that it might do this for a few days before it gave up the ghost.

While the snake was doing its thing, two large iron kettles bubbled over open fires, full of fresh hog and deer meat, potatoes and onions. It smelled good. The deer's head was swinging on a string from the porch roof. I didn't see the hog's head swinging anywhere so I guessed it was in the pot. (Uh oh, where was that rattlesnake's head?)

Our host, Ray, offered us mixed drinks of vodka and Hawaiian Punch. I wanted to retain use of my faculties, so I chose a less potent beverage. It's a good thing, because later I ended up in Ray's cherry tree, which was chock full of the juicy red fruits. I picked two quarts out there by myself. Hey, I never claimed to be much fun at parties.

There were lots of other activities going on—guitar playing, volley-ball, horseshoes, and a basketball game that looked more like a wrestling match. The game had no rules, no fouls or penalties. I noticed and made a comment that some of the participants were bleeding. Sam (a Steam Hollow native) proudly informed me, "That's not basket-ball—that's hollerball."

As country music (I would name the singers to be more specific, but I don't know one from the other) blared from a pickup truck, I wondered what would happen if I changed it to a rock and roll station like WWWV. Confidentially, I hate (yes, hate is the right word) country music. I equate it with scratching chalk on a blackboard, eating liver, undergoing a root canal, dissecting frogs or riding through New Jersey with my windows open. To make it worse, during some of the key Most Horrible Moments of My Life, country music has been playing.

The radio was turned off when the a-pickin' and a-grinnin' began. I do play the guitar, but since I've never tried the boing-twang-boing-twang stuff, I didn't volunteer my talents. Would you believe they asked me, a bona fide, died-in-the-wool, arrogant, know-it-all Yankee, to sing? This was a most gracious gesture of Southern hospitality.

"Can you play 'How Does It Feel to be One of the Beautiful People?'" I asked. This did not compute. They began without me.

By the time the meat and vegetables were heaped onto platters, everyone was hungry. The enthusiasm for this meal, which was killed and butchered by Ray and his friends, reminded me of the seafood feasts I enjoyed "back home" on Long Island. Those who made their living off the Great South Bay would bring clams, crabs and lobsters to bake, boil and grill. I thought about inviting these holler folks to a clambake someday to reciprocate the cultural experience.

At a clambake, hot coals are spread across the bottom of a wide hole. Then the clams, crabs and/or lobsters are put in, and buried to bake for hours. Mmmmm. But I don't know if these people would like that kind of food. I don't know if I could ever afford it.

For now, I wonder if I'll get invited to any more parties. Maybe at the next one I can pick string beans.

Other Places, Other Ways

There are so many other places to be.

As I drove the country road to work Tuesday, the mist veiled the foot of the distant mountains. The nearer hills rippled like gentle round waves. At my left, thousands of wet young corn blades glittered in the sun.

The dashboard clock said 7:55 a.m. My best friend would now be on the subway to downtown Boston. I went with her in my mind, as I had in deed two mornings before, down the hole on the squealing escalator to the dank tunnel. A young child of perhaps 3 had kicked and screamed that day, her refusal reminding us that humans were not naturally inclined to this.

Like the New York subway system, everything in Boston—walls, floor, signs, benches—is coated with filth and smells of unwashed humanity. My friend misses living in the Valley, and I wish for her not always to long for it, but to carry it with her.

There are so many other places to be. It helps sometimes to go see them.

The day before Boston, my husband and I had been in Northampton, Mass., to witness my brother's wedding. The ceremony was held at the Unitarian Society church. It was a very different sort of church and ceremony than I'd ever experienced. There was no cross. No talk of Jesus Christ. And no talk of God.

But there was much talk of Spirit and love and promises. I found I could respect that. And, believe me, there was a time when I would not have. When I would have brushed it off—and so my brother and his bride—as not valid.

It took a long time for my brother to come to this place, to be able to step into a church, to look into a woman's eyes and say these things, to make these promises. He's 38, and you might say, well, it's about time. But that's how much time it took.

At the reception, my place at the table was between the aunts of my youth, one from each side of my family and now from opposite coasts of Florida. After salad was served, I poured on the dressing and began to pick at the broccoli. Aunt Joyce said, "I don't think we're supposed to start eating yet, Luanne."

When the dressing was passed to Uncle Dick (Joyce's husband), he refused dutifully and waited. Meanwhile, most of us at the table and around the room ate. About 15 minutes later, our waiter told us, "After you're done with your salad, you can help yourself to the buffet." A look passed between my aunt and uncle, and he asked for the dressing.

For Aunt Joyce, appearances are everything. The family must maintain an aura of impeccability. Lacking that, we must have explanations, even if they are wrong. We have no skeletons. Heck, we don't even have closets.

I asked Aunt Clara, who still has her thick German accent, about Bike Week at Daytona Beach, Fla., since she lives just a few miles from there. Could we stay with her and Uncle Bob if we came down?

She said, "You ride on the back of that Harley with him (referring to my husband)?"

"Yeah, it's fun," I said.

"Luanne!" she said indignantly.

When I was a child Aunt Clara told me, "A lady is supposed to always sit with her legs together, no matter what she's wearing." For Aunt Clara, everything is black or white. Unlike Aunt Joyce, she needs no consensus to know what she thinks. She expresses her opinions loudly and forcefully.

Each of my aunts has found a way to keep life orderly and sane.

After the reception we drove to Boston. Before my friend came to the Valley to attend college, she'd lived in Boston all her life. She'd known the same streets and houses, the same friends and family, the same beliefs and behaviors, all her life. When she returned "home" a year ago, she was a very different person than the one who'd left four years earlier.

To paraphrase Gerald May, M.D., in his book, "Will And Spirit," we who are seekers need a location, a place, a framework, from which to leave and return, or, he warns, "it is too easy to wander aimlessly. But when the location becomes exclusive and self-identifying, the search is lost altogether."

There are so many other places to be. It is good to go see them. It is good to come home.

A Place for Me

I like it better here than Long Island.

This occurs to me while driving the back roads of the Shenandoah Valley. Even after 23 years of living here, I have not tired of the scenery: of Angus herds grazing on a grassy slope, of patchwork fields sliced by spring-fed creeks, of weathered gray barns bursting with round bales of hay.

Long Island, a big suburb of New York City, is such a distant memory.

There's not much to miss about Long Island anymore. Not bagels or pizza or egg rolls. Most of the foods I first missed are available here now. If not, I can live without them on a daily basis.

Save the eating of knishes and stuffed cabbage and antipasto for vacations.

I do not miss shopping or concerts or things to do. What's so great about being clad in the latest styles? I like nothing better than to sit on my back deck watching the sun set over my neighbor's horse pasture, unless it's walking down our dirt road along the Middle River.

All I miss is the water and beaches. Growing up, my sense of direction was defined by the Long Island Sound directly north and the Great South Bay and Atlantic Ocean directly south. On the island, you could only go so far until you hit a watery boundary.

It took years to get re-oriented, to know where I am by new perimeters and parameters—the Blue Ridge Mountains to the east and Appalachians to the west.

The water was always a place of spiritual retreat, too: a place to run to, to be alone or alone with God. The horizon was water and sky to eternity.

Now I lift up my eyes to the hills, from where my help comes. The mountains are more graspable, definable, solid. They may not be eternal, but they are ancient, majestic and…there.

I have only to stroll up the hill behind my house to see all three mountain ranges.

We have 12 acres with two ponds. Before we bought this place seven years ago, we had a place in the mountains (which I miss)—11 acres with our very own woods and barn, spring and stream.

On Long Island, the best I could have hoped for was one of Pete Seeger's ticky tacky little boxes. The environment I fled consisted of endless housing developments and streets lined with shopping plaza after shopping plaza, punctuated every few feet by yet another traffic light.

Yes, the valley is becoming like that, but at least between towns there are still wide-open spaces. Let's hope our county planners appreciate the aesthetic and environmental value of the farmland and not just the resources it holds for making money.

Long Island was not always like that. A few potato farms remain to testify of what was once life-giving farmland—the topsoil beneath the pavement and concrete is unsurpassed in its loaminess. A few unpolluted spots in the bay remain to testify of the once-thriving clamming and fishing communities along the coast.

My brother and sisters all bailed out, too. We grew up in a small town on the bay where Grandpa owned the tiny grocery store. Our aunts, uncles and cousins all lived within a few miles of each other. Some of them are still there, but all that remains of our immediate family's existence on Long Island is headstones.

You won't find my family's name in the history records of the Shenandoah Valley. We have no headstones here, no "home place" to return to, no great-grands who were kicked off the park or who founded a church or business.

Yet my children have known no other way of life. They have grown up hiking the mountains, wading the creeks and gazing at the black skies on a starlit night in the Shenandoah Valley. They don't know what it's like to lock the doors of everything coming and going or to be accosted by perverts on the street. No, I do not miss Long Island, only the way it used to be.

And I hope to never have to say that about the Shenandoah Valley.

Behind These Doors

○ ○

What if we thought of the family less as the determining influence by which we are formed and more the raw material from which we can make a life?

—Thomas Moore

A Valentine Test of Love

It was the perfect Valentine's Day. Right.

I've always believed Valentine's Day to be one of those "Hallmark holidays" specifically designed to get consumers to consume during the mid-winter consumption lull, but in recent years it's become an opportunity for me to express my affection for members of my family. In small ways.

I had it all planned, complete with a delicious family meal.

My first gift was for my dearest love, my husband. I've learned a few things over the years and one of those things is that although men have their romantic flowers-and-candy moments, for the most part they perceive love as expressed in practical ways. So while he was yet asleep, I took our car down to our local tire mart and had all its threadbare tires replaced.

Next I bought some token gifts at my favorite store for Valentine's Day, the Augusta Cooperative Farm Bureau. Granted, the selection is limited, but what they have is lovely. I bought a small stuffed monkey (that resembled Curious George) and dog (that resembled Wishbone) for the boys, and two delicate teacup holders with candles for the girls.

These gifts were going to be set on each dinner plate.

My dinner plans included a golden roast chicken surrounded by saffron rice and, for dessert, a white cake with cherries between the three layers, iced with creamy chocolate.

Back home, I mixed the cake and set the three round pans in the oven.

The phone rang. It was the elementary school, saying my grandson had a stomachache and a low fever. I had to go get him.

On my way out the door I asked, "Rachel, can you rotate the layers in the oven in about five minutes and take them out at 11:40?"

"No problem," said Rachel.

When I returned home, the storm door was propped open. Uh oh. Something had burned. One of the layers had spilled all over the oven bottom, Rachel said. The other two had to be removed prematurely.

OK. Forget the cake.

Awhile later, my husband asked if I wanted to take an hour-long motorcycle ride. Sure. As we left, knowing an hour in his time is two hours on the clock, I said to Rachel, "If I'm not back by 4 o'clock, can you put the chicken in the oven at 400 degrees?"

"No problem," said Rachel.

We had a lovely ride. When I walked back in the house at 4:40 p.m., the chicken was still on the counter. I said nothing, just stuck it in a pan and shoved it in the oven.

Soon the oven began smoking. She hadn't cleaned it. I opened the door to remove the chicken and the oven was on fire. I grabbed a canister and threw about two pounds of flour on the flames. Successfully smothered.

OK. Forget the chicken.

When Rachel came into the kitchen, ready to go out, I told her she wasn't going anywhere until she cleaned out the oven.

"Use the shop vac to get the flour out," I said. "It's down in the basement."

As Rachel vacuumed the oven, flour spewed out the vacuum's top vent, leaving a fine dusting of white on the counters, table, chairs…just about half the kitchen.

When she left, Rachel said, "You're welcome."

I wasn't sure what she meant by that. What was I supposed to thank her for?

Later, Rachel told me she had met some friends at Waffle House and told them she'd had a tiff with me before leaving home. They were extremely interested in this, wondering what I had done to her. Rachel wondered why they were so interested, until they pointed out that she, too, was covered with flour.

Back home, I was relieved that Rachel was out of the house. I was able to salvage the sad remaining cake layers, covering them with chocolate icing. As my older daughter, Heidi, cut a slice later, she knocked her cake plate to the floor. It smashed. Some of the flying pieces landed with a poof into the flour still on the floor.

I looked at the incident, then resumed eating my cake. My grandson, 6, said, "Aren't you going to yell at her? She should be in big, big trouble."

Heidi and I could not help but laugh. "Happy Valentine's day," I said.

The Bright Stuff

I am so proud of him.

My brother, at 39, is graduating in a few weeks from the University of Massachusetts with a bachelor's degree in English. What makes me so proud is the obstacles he had to overcome on his way to this degree.

The biggest one being he's stupid.

At least that's what Dad always told him. It stopped Kevin from taking any college preparation classes in high school. Resigning himself to a life of skilled labor, he decided then to enroll in VOCES, the local vocational technical school.

"That's for dummies," Dad told him. So Kevin graduated from high school with no skills and worked in various factories for a few years before enlisting in the U.S. Marines.

When he came out, he had a skill and got a job at Sikorsky installing, updating and repairing helicopter electronics. Since he was the best at what he did, he was paid well for it. He liked the money but grew to hate the job.

During a major family and, in turn, personal crisis, Kevin started attending meetings for Adult Children of Alcoholics (ACOA). That's when he learned that Dad—and Mom—may not have nurtured him in the most healthy ways. And that their take on life and on him may not have been entirely accurate.

Kevin did something radical for a person who has always believed he was stupid: he began to take college classes part-time. He started with psychology-related classes but once he'd worked through most of his "issues," dumped them in favor of subjects that genuinely interested him.

He bought bookcases and has slowly filled them with literature present and past; his rock-and-roll albums were joined by the jazz and classical works he began to enjoy; he decorated his walls with his own framed black-and-white photographs.

He started running, became a vegetarian and lost a hundred pounds. He also learned to contra dance. He found it difficult to continue hanging around with old friends whose only interest was drinking beer and smoking cigarettes and whining.

After a lifetime of infrequent dating because of the unhealthy way he related to women, he met his future wife at a contra dance convention and married her last June.

Kevin is an exception, I think. I know few people who are willing to relinquish the memories of a normal and happy childhood to deal with the behind-the-scenes abuse and craziness. Most folks stay in the same groove throughout their lives.

Experts say that children who are berated and belittled by their parents show the same symptoms as children who are physically or sexually abused—feeling bad about themselves, doing poorly in school, using drugs, having trouble making friends, getting depressed.

Sticks and stones break bones and names hurt. Some parents seem to think they can shame their children into behaving well by calling them stupid or lazy or selfish. Some do it by belittling the child in front of others.

Children are not lesser beings. They need to be respected just as any human does. That means if a kid spills his milk at the dinner table you don't go into a big tirade about what a clumsy idiot the kid is. Remember that you sometimes spill things too: how do you like to be treated when that happens?

The Golden Rule helps here. Do unto others what you would have others do unto you.

God spoke and the world was created and he saw that it was good. What we are creating in our children will stay with them for a lifetime.

My sister-in-law told me, "I don't think Kevin knows how bright he is." That's a demon he'll probably always struggle with.

Kevin told me not long ago that he and our sisters say I'm the smartest in the bunch. They only believe that because Dad told everyone how brilliant I was growing up. Dad said I was going to be the first woman president of the U.S. and bought me books and magazines that were way over my head.

I never could live up to the intellectual level Dad thought I had reached, but I sure worked at it. And so I too felt like a failure.

Maybe if Dad had taken the care to get to know each of us, what our innate gifts were, our desires and sources of motivation and enjoyment, and nurtured that, we would not have had to suffer so as adults to find our place.

However, in *Care of the Soul*, Thomas Moore points out, "What if we thought of the family less as the determining influence by which we are formed and more the raw material from which we can make a life?"

Yes. I'm sure my brother would agree.

A Knead to Bake Bread

No matter how often I bake bread for my family, it is always a treat.

Such a plain thing, bread is, such a plain ordinary thing.

Time was, when the children were young, that I baked all our bread. Always I had to make at least three loaves at a time. The first loaf was gobbled up as it came out of the oven. The second was often to give away. So our home was filled with the smell of bread baking twice a week.

I bought grains—whole wheat flour, unbleached white flour and oats—in 50 pound bags through a food co-op.

During this season of my life, time does not allow me to bake bread that often. Inspiration hits when I wake up to the first chill of autumn, a snow storm or a rainy day.

"I have to bake bread today," I think.

What I want is to have my hands in the warm dough kneading, while looking out the window at the gray sky not thinking. Or while conversing with my grandson or a daughter. Or while thinking about a problem I'm trying to work out.

What I want is for loved ones to come in from the cold and smell the bread and know that this is home and that I love them.

I sprinkle flour on my four-square-foot bread board, then knead it into the forming dough. The ball starts off as a blob of ingredients—flour, yeast, salt, honey, oil, water—but as I knead, its texture changes.

Knead, turn, fold, knead, turn, fold, knead, turn, fold, knead, turn, fold, knead, turn, fold…

When I was younger—in my 20s—I was rather rough with dough, imitating the only bread makers I'd ever seen, the Italian men who made pizza dough in restaurants. While talking in a loud stream of Italian, they slammed the dough, slammed the dough, slammed the dough onto the board.

I tend to be gentle, not wanting to break it or tear its fibers, and firm, pushing it towards its destiny.

Knead, turn, fold, knead, turn, fold. Beneath my fingers, in the grip of my hand, I feel it transform into a smooth, pliable mass. There should be a word for dough that is perfectly ready to rise.

This knowing when it's ready is something you learn to know as you do it again and again. At first you follow the directions: "Knead for eight minutes." But later, when you know dough, you just knead until it's time to stop.

The little fella goes into a bowl and covered with a clean dish towel. I got the "little fella" expression from the Dunbar gals. They're the ones who taught me to bake bread.

When my family and I moved to Virginia in 1978, buying Italian bread or stone-ground whole-wheat bread meant a trip to Harrisonburg from my apartment in Shenandoah. It was out of necessity that I made an attempt at making a loaf—verily a disgusting experience.

After an instructional and hilarious afternoon in the Dunbar kitchen, I tried again. The resulting loaves of French bread were not perfect, but much better. Edible was the goal.

When it's about doubled in size, I push my fist into the airy dough, cut it in half with a long serrated knife, roll each half out, shape them into loaves to rise again, then place them into a warm oven.

When we lived in the hollow, heating the oven was an art in itself, seein's how it was a wood cook stove.

That's right. Our house in the hollow came with a wood cook stove in the kitchen, and it was great for baking bread. The shelf over the range top stayed warm all the time, so rising the dough there was wonderful.

It was a bit of work, getting the oven to the right temperature and maintaining it there. Sometimes it was up and down a bit. You had to open and close not only the top flue, but also dampers for air channels in the stove that controlled circulation. And then you had to rotate the baking loaves periodically because the oven was warmest by the firebox side.

I take the loaves from the oven when I suspect they're done. Immediately I roll one onto the counter. I inspect the bottom to be sure it is brownish and hard, not doughy-looking or soft. I flick it to listen for a hollow sound.

After just a few minutes, it's ready for the knife. No butter necessary. As my tasters' mouths are filled with their first bite, they moan with pleasure.

Such a plain thing, bread is, such a plain ordinary thing.

There is so much beauty in bread—
Beauty of sun and soil,
Beauty of patient toil.
Winds and rain have caressed it,
Christ often blessed it.
Be gentle when you touch bread.

—Unknown

Cleaning the Mess

Well, it's over.

For four years, I had no answer. I asked women and men, old and young, homemakers and shopkeepers. In hushed voice I pulled people aside and asked for advice, nodding with hope with each new solution.

But trying their suggestions—some radical—yielded no improvement. I spent a lot of time on my knees, to no avail. As the years went by and the situation grew worse, I became self-conscious about it, paranoid that it was glaring to others. I was ashamed, but there was no longer a way to hide it. I stopped getting down on my knees and gave up.

Then a few weeks ago, a friend—a certified professional—came to visit. She gave me some good no-nonsense counsel.

Thank you, I said, feeling hopeful for the first time in years. She sounded so sure of herself.

So last week, when nobody else was home, I spent six hours on my knees, working on the problem. And now I can say, with no conflict of conscience, with total joy, that...my kitchen floor is clean.

You laugh, you who have not had the responsibility of keeping a floor clean for years and years, through blizzards and rain, Kool-Aid and mustard, dribbling babies and basketballs.

A floor that gets dirtier and dirtier and dirtier, no matter how much you clean it, can weigh heavily upon a person. No darn kidding. I got to where I wouldn't invite anyone over and if someone did come over, I visited with them out on the porch. For me, who has entertained hundreds of people in my home over the years, that's pretty bad.

The off-white floor began to soil shortly after we moved in, its pale peach flowers and green leaves lined with just a teensy bit of grime. Scrubbing didn't make it go away. After a few months the whole floor was dingy.

I tried Murphy's Oil Soap, plain soap, Mr. Clean, Pine Sol, Fantastic, Ajax, Windex, to name a few. Then, later, as the condition of the floor worsened, the abrasives—ammonia, bleach. First diluted, then straight.

I did everything but follow the manufacturer's instructions. That's for people who cannot think for themselves. Their products are a rip-off. I can find a better, cheaper way to do it.

Yeah, a way that doesn't work. After awhile, scrubbing became so frustrating I stopped doing it and began using a mop-and-wax type product. "No rinsing!"

No, no rinsing. Just push the dirt around and wax over it. The shine distracted the eye from the dirt beneath. As my friend Cindy so aptly put it: dirt, wax, dirt, wax, dirt, wax.

I thought about those layers of dirt and wax yesterday, when someone said to me that families keep their secrets for years and just cover them up and go on.

It's true. You hear people sometimes speak of the dead as though they were saints all their lives when you know the guy was anything but. And so the dirt is sealed with the heavy wax of denial, ensuring that the sins are passed to the next generation.

The same is true of individuals and institutions. Appearances are everything. Distract the eye from the dirt. Survival is construed as keeping the image intact whatever the cost.

We've seen it in the President of the United States: Exploiting and abusing the women in his life—the sex partners, his daughter, his wife—while representing himself as a champion of women's rights. And so we as women have had to decide, do we want our floor clean? Do we want men to truly respect women? Or do we want superficial laws enacted to make it appear that we're respected?

And we see it in our own lives: Tell a white lie, pass on gossip, keep the mistaken extra change, scream at our children, belittle our spouses, lust for what's not good for us. The accumulated dirt of everyday traffic.

And every day justifying: He does it to me all the time, people need to be warned about her, their prices are a rip-off anyway, the kid wouldn't listen to me, he/she needs to change, I've always been like this. The wax.

While timeworn excuses may help us—as an individual, family, institution—fool ourselves, the accumulated dirt beneath the cheesy shine eventually becomes glaring to others.

A quote I saw yesterday on a sign said something like this: "Some men will look everywhere for answers but the Bible."—Napoleon.

The manufacturer's instructions tell us to confess and be forgiven, to go to those we've offended, that following truth will alone set us free. And there's only one product that gets our conscience clean.

Got Those Shopping Day Blues

It starts with a comment, grows to a chant and finally swells to a roar:

"I'm hungry."

"There's nothing to eat."

"Mom, when are you going food shopping?"

I have put it off for days, maybe a week, and now we have no jelly, no ketchup, and no butter. We've eaten chicken for dinner three times in the past week (cooked differently each time, hoping they won't realize it's chicken). We're using napkins for toilet paper. We've fed the cat all the tuna fish.

So I study the grocery store ads. Wow, chopped meat (hamburger to y'all) is only 98 cents at one store and round roast is $1.58. I like the produce at this place, too, so I decide to go there. Good thing it's not a Monster Store.

Those Monster Stores overwhelm me. I'm more of a short-term-goal person. I don't want to trek through aisles of outdoor furniture, jewelry, pets, clothing and books in search of the food. Grocery shopping must be achievable to me—an errand, not an expedition.

If I had my druthers, I'd do all my shopping at this little owner-operated store around the corner from my house. I stop there every other day for milk and bread, sale items, snacks and stuff-I-run-out-of. But the selection is limited and the prices are generally higher. Even so, I have this theory that my money has more value there because it's more valued by the folks who run the store and work there.

My hard-earned cash is not disappearing into some humongous corporate account, but actually feeding and clothing them: the owner who greets me with a smile, the middle-aged blond cashier who chats with me about the weather, the boy who carries my bags out to the car.

Not today. Today my first stop is the cheap-o bargain store, where I buy two or three months' worth of dish and laundry detergents and other cleaning and hygiene supplies. Name-brand products are so cheap here I can afford to stock up.

Next, the bread store, where I buy two loaves for the price of one. My family eats whole-grain breads, which cost more than the white Styrofoam variety. I've never understood why. Doesn't it cost the mills more to a.) sift the nutritious bran and germ from the flour, b.) bleach the natural color and remaining vitamins and minerals out of it and c.) add a few artificial B vitamins back in?

Next is the grocery store. Pots of chrysanthemums and hanging houseplants seduce me into the produce department. I hear a "ssshhhh" as a mist sprays the fresh romaine, chicory and Boston lettuces, the red, leafy radishes, the purple-edged turnips, and a profusion of other colorful vegetables. A wren flies overhead.

The tropical rain forest atmosphere of this place seems like the bird's natural environment. I turn to the woman shopping beside me and ask, "Is this part of the decor?" We laugh as a clerk dashes past us in pursuit of the happy bird.

I pick a zucchini, green and black-mottled, off a neatly stacked row. "Hmm, it looks fresh," I think. "Let's give it the old fresh-test." My method of checking zucchini is to grasp it firmly at one end, turn it upright and wiggle it. If it jiggles like rubber—NG—no good. This one is good. No jiggle.

I wish I could buy all the fruit the government says we should eat. The USDA tells us to eat two fresh fruits a day. There are six people in my house. Two fruits times six people times seven days equals 84 pieces of fruit. Gosh, where would I put it all? I settle for a dozen each of apples, oranges and bananas.

I head to the meat cases and get lots of this 98 cent chopped meat to make into burgers. I don't eat it because of my cholesterol. But my husband, who thinks nothing of loading a small mountain of bacon, greasy onions and Cheddar cheese on that burger, has consistently low cholesterol.

In the frozen-food section, a man takes an item from the case and puts it in the cart. His wife picks it up and examines the carton. "Too much fat!" she says, and puts it back. I witness this scene two more times with this couple. Poor fellow. I think, "Either she's saving his life or she's a USDA drone."

I have to laugh, as I wheel down the snack aisles, at some of the junk food they're offering us these days: fat-free potato chips (yuck), fat-free cookies, fat-free cakes, fat-free ice cream. Does anyone besides me remember when not so long ago, sugar was the insidious destroyer of life? Now it's fine, just fine, to eat all the sugar you want, as long as there's no fat in it. Or when oat bran was added to everything? This single non-nutrient was the key to preventing cancer, losing weight, clearing up acne and extending your life. How much is the Brooklyn Bridge selling for these days?

I go through my ritual of staring at the ice cream—my Achilles' heel. There's my favorite, rocky road. I could buy it "for the kids," but I know I'll eat most of it. With a sigh, I push my overloaded cart to the checkout.

When I get home, two kids take over and put all the groceries away. That's nice; they're also inspecting to see if I've gotten what they've asked for and to check for any surprises.

All is well, until, about a week from now I hear a voice from the kitchen: "Mom! There's nothing to eat."

Keeping Promises

I was 18; he was 20.

We promised to stay together for the rest of our lives. To love, honor and cherish every day from now on until we die.

How could we see that far ahead? We couldn't possibly know what those promises would mean 10 years, 20 years, 30 years from then.

Neither of us is the same person we were 25 years ago when we stood before the witnesses and said, "I do." Just making that commitment changes you. Food shopping together changes you. Being parents changes you. Growing up changes you.

Soon after the wedding on Aug. 25, 1974, the new husband was unemployed. In those days, lots of people were unemployed. Me, I was pregnant. It never occurred to me to look for a job.

We had no car, no telephone. Our furniture was scavenged: an orange vinyl chair, a floral loveseat, a Formica table.

I knew how to cook spaghetti, potato salad and meat loaf. That was it. On our "budget," we ate the same things over and over: spaghetti, chicken and hot dogs. Later I learned about beans and rice.

For our first Christmas together, the husband gave me cake pans and a photo album. The photo album, OK, but at 19 I was not ready for a lifetime of gifts like blenders, toasters and Tupperware. The next year I got perfume.

We decorated our tree with day-glow ornaments we made ourselves, illuminated by our six-foot black light. Psychedelic. The relatives were tactful: How…um, original.

It was our tree and we thought it was beautiful.

After the baby came, the grandparents and other relatives made sure she lacked nothing. Heidi had more dresses than she ever wore. I wore hand-me-downs from my younger sisters.

Each of our upbringings brought us into marriage with various confusing expectations. Neither of us had any idea of how to deal with conflict. Our role models taught us how to yell, scream, attack, drink, overeat, smoke, sulk, threaten, slam, wheel out.

We're still learning how to disagree like intelligent human beings who love each other.

Love means saying you're sorry when you've hurt the one you love most in the world. Whose good grace is most important? Harsh and hurting words piled one on top of the other that are never taken back go on hurting and go on hurting.

My boss, Richard Morin, and his wife will soon celebrate their 46th anniversary. This is what he told me: "We never went to bed without kissing. No matter what was going on, we kissed each other good night."

Romantic? Perhaps. But that kiss is filled with meaning. It means that no matter what, I still love you.

How you treat the one you live with till death is more important than how you treat anyone else in the world, including your boss, your secretary, the grocery store clerk.

A male acquaintance told me that in counseling (which they sought too late), his wife said he was so attentive and animated when he spoke with other women. He told me she was a jealous person and I asked, "Are you still attentive and animated with her?"

It is good to seek help if you're in over your head. So many of us are hardened into patterns of relating with our spouses that we cannot see any other way. It can be a counselor or a friend. Anyone who's a good listener, with a marriage you admire (or single, as long as they're not hurting from a divorce), of the same sex as you, who has a different perspective.

Since it is impossible to change another person, the question is never, "When will he/she ever change?" but, "How do I need to change?"

The husband and I moved here to Virginia four years into the marriage. Without our moms and dads nearby, nor brothers and sisters and friends, we had no one but each other. That's when we became friends and truly married to each other. Not without some adjustment problems, but even so.

So Tuesday we celebrate our 25th anniversary. In that time I have learned that the feelings of love come and go and come back again, it can be easier being poor together than being prosperous and that living with someone day in day out causes you to know the good, the bad and the ugly of them.

There is no big secret to staying married for a lifetime. It's not easy, but it is simple.

Just keep your wedding day promises: love, honor and cherish until death.

All in a Day

A whole day awaits, clear and free.

I drink my coffee in the dusk of sunrise. In the quiet, I look forward to all the day holds. I can do so much today and do nothing. I have time for both.

What do I want to do?

Mop the kitchen floor, vacuum the living room, wash the storm door windows; call a friend, take a long walk, write a column; hang the sheets on the line, bake some French bread, sweep the decks and porch.

The house stirs as family members emerge from their rooms. The husband and I discuss upcoming motorcycle tours, while Heidi gets ready for work, Patrick for school. Just before the bus arrives, there is a mini-frenzy—locating socks and shoes, turning the red jacket right-side-out and adjusting the backpack—and then Patrick is out the door.

Customers—two British fellows—are arriving this morning, so I run the vacuum around the back room. Load the washer with towels. It's 8:30.

Time to exercise. I do the upper body stuff while the husband wipes down his motorcycle. Move towels from washer to dryer, put sheets in washer. Make a fruit and protein shake for breakfast.

Rachel emerges and we talk about her upcoming day.

At 9:30 the customers arrive. The husband pulls out their motorcycle of choice for a once-over while I process the fellows' paperwork. Funny and interesting chaps, from the Isle of Wight off England's southern coast.

I envy the husband spending the whole day riding with these guys. But I had decided not to go so as to have the whole day to "get things done."

As they leave at 10:30, the telephone rings. It's Rachel and she wants to talk to Kelli, her sleepover guest who's still here.

I hang out the sheets, then begin exercising the lower body stuff. I gulp down a glass of water. Kelli asks if I want to see photos of Josh and Joanie's wedding that my kids also attended. She goes out to her car to get the photos.

While waiting, I think about all the stuff I have to do today and that this is not on my list. A half-sentence floats into my consciousness, something I heard recently about "wasting time together." Kelli is one of those like-part-of-the-family friends.

We look at the pictures, then talk about her wedding plans. She describes the gown she wants, and I agree to make it for her.

The business phone rings. A fellow from Alexandria wants to join a motorcycle tour Saturday on the Blue Ridge Parkway. We exchange all the necessary info in about 20 minutes.

It's noon when Kelli leaves. OK. The day awaits. Well, half of it. I decide to call Margie because we've both been so busy lately that we hardly ever talk and I miss her.

At 12:30 I sit down to write, deciding to take that long walk and vacuum when my back needs relief from sitting. At 1 the mail arrives, so I dash out to the box to retrieve it, give it a once over, return to my desk.

Heidi gets home at 1:30. We talk for a bit and I decide it's time for my three-mile walk. A wind is pulling a curtain of clouds over the sky's blueness, and I hope it does not rain on my motorcyclists.

I wish I could get paid to walk. It's 2 p.m. Wednesday. Farmers are cutting corn, planes are flying overhead, women and men dash up and down the road and I am taking a walk. A tractor passes, pulling some sort of cutting attachment. The driver, enclosed in a cab, veers left, then turns right into a field of tan and brown corn stalks.

On the other side of this rolling field, off in the distance, another tractor is pulling an enclosed wagon attachment. Perhaps collecting the chopped silage. It will take a few days to cut and collect this whole field.

You don't hear about farmers becoming serial killers. They don't have time. They're too busy surviving. When they're not working they're thinking about what they must do tomorrow and next week and next spring. Serial killers must be bored.

It's nearly three when I return and make juice of carrots, celery and apples for me and Heidi. As we sit and talk about her job, her moving out, her wedding, I think this is not on my list. But this doesn't happen just any old day, just sitting around in the afternoon drinking carrot juice and sharing dreams.

I come back to the writing. Patrick comes home and it's time to start the French breadmaking process. Of course he wants to help.

As the afternoon closes, I review my "to do" list. It happens every week: the kitchen floor and window washing must wait. In a book I read once about getting organized, the authors pointed out that, when we moms are dead and gone, we will not be remembered for our clean houses, but for our kindness and care for those we love.

And that is my excuse.

Well, It Takes Patience

I've discovered the wonderful world of Styrofoam. Which at this point in human achievement does not include Styrofoam mixing bowls.

Since our well dried up near the end of the drought and subsequently, the pump burnt out, we have been eating from Styrofoam plates, slurping from Styrofoam bowls and drinking from Styrofoam cups. And since our water isn't running, we are.

Running to the homes of friends and relatives to take showers, to the grocery store for bottled water, to the community spring to fetch tanks of water, to the tank to fetch a pail of water and to the pail to fill the pot.

It's been a month. Yes, we have contracted with a man to drill a new well, but he's been busy with another job and we are the very picture of patience.

Someone right away lent us a 350-gallon tank, which is on the back of our six-wheel truck parked by the back door. So we fetch it from the truck in our five-gallon Hebrew National buckets. No one's fallen down and broken their crown, but my back is creaking.

Did you know it takes five gallons of water to flush the toilet?

Anyway, showers are now social events. That's getting to be a hassle. The other morning I threw all my toiletries and clothes into a bag to take a shower at Margie's and about two miles from the house realized I forgot to pack a bra. Not something I would or could prevail upon her to lend me.

A friend suggested putting pins in a map tracking where we've all taken showers. I've taken two at the Talley's (my daughter's friend's house), three or four at my friend Margie's and one at my brother-in-law's. If we don't drill soon, we'll have to widen our circle of friends.

When I don't "bathe out" the process at home is just as time-consuming. Although I must say I've gotten the ritual down to about three gallons total of water. That's washing and conditioning the hair, washing my body and shaving my legs.

We went to the Health Department to get a permit to drill. You can't drill within 100 feet of the septic system, 100 feet from where the animals (in this case cows and goat) congregate and 50 feet from the foundation of the house if it's been treated for termites.

That, by the way, was a wonderful revelation, since the well we've been drinking from for the past four years is under the house, so it's likely contaminated.

Someone gave me a copy of an article on "witching" and I thought, I'm a sensitive intuitive type, so I tried it. I broke a branch into the Y shape and walked around the yard trying to be sensitive, open, to the twitching of the stick, but nothing happened.

It was quite arrogant of me to think I could just go out there and do it. The people who succeed at dousing claim to be gifted in some way.

We just picked a convenient spot between the house and the barn. So we've got the spot and we wait. The reason I don't just go ahead and get someone else to drill is because of the honesty I sense in the guy with whom we have a verbal contract. I believe if he finds enough water at 80 feet he will not continue on to 400 feet so he can make more money.

In the meantime, we continue to make the rounds of shower locations, eat our pot pies, frozen dinners and packaged salads and boil water to wash our faces. It's inconvenient, but it's not a hardship.

I mean, things could be a lot worse.

So I've gained this great appreciation for running water and have learned to make do with little of it. But when the well project is finished we're having a big water party.

This is my big fantasy:

We'll do load after load of laundry all day and boil pounds and pounds of macaroni and dirty all the pots and pans and plates and silverware. We'll run the shower continuously and just go in there and get wet whenever we feel like it even if we're not dirty.

And the sound of the dishwasher will be heard far into the night.

Silent Night, Waterless Night—With 'No-Well'

It was Christmas Eve. The gently-lit church sanctuary glittered here and there with gay lights and the smiles of excited children.

"Noel, noel, noel, noel…" sang the congregation.

My husband and I turned to each other, writhing at the words. "No well, no well, no well, no well…" we sang. Our well had gone dry Oct. 5, and here it was, Dec. 24, two months and two weeks later, and we were still without water.

It was to last three months and 10 days. The whole time thinking it would be just a few more days. If I'd known at the start how long it would take…what would I have done?

At first we spiritualized it. Ah yes, it represented this time in our lives when our spiritual well had dried up and we needed to look to new sources, as we were in our physical yard, from which to draw refreshment for our souls.

Yeah, yeah, yeah, OK. That lasted about three days.

I reminded myself of all the people in the world, far from here, who had to walk five miles daily to fill their clay pots with water. I'm not one of those spoiled rich Americans, I told myself.

We were hanging in there with the well driller, who happened upon a season of bad luck starting when he met us (hmmm). We'd made a verbal contract with the fellow about a week into our crisis. He thought his present project would take just a few more days.

As it happened, he was boring through rock, and the few days stretched to a few more days…and a few more…until it was a whole month before he brought his drill here.

When he began to drill, something broke. I never did find out just what, but it was something important because he left with a part off his rig, leaving the rest anchored into my yard.

"They only made 12 of these," he said of his machine.

So the parts had to be manufactured and shipped from somewhere far away. More days stretched into more weeks. And the weeks stretched to months.

In the meantime, we ate and drank from Styrofoam, hauling water in buckets from the tank in the yard to the house to wash with. Taking showers at friends', doing wash at the laundromat. It got old.

Most of the time I endured patiently and with a sense of humor and a transcendent perspective, wearing my martyrdom lightly. But one week I got so tired of arranging, packing and traveling for a shower. Nor did I want to lug in the buckets and boil water to wash myself.

Five days went by.

Finally, on a cold Saturday morning, I took a towel and some shampoo out to the truck in the yard and washed my hair at the tank. It was coooold.

I felt better once my hair was clean.

But things got really bad one Wednesday. My daughter called me at work and said the septic had backed up. It was bad.

It was really bad.

We spent about $50 on "snakes" to clean it, but nothing worked. The next morning we called a septic guy and sat around talking about where we were going to live until we had water and septic again.

It was afternoon when the septic guy finally came. After he got it fixed, we all rejoiced, and the lack of water didn't bother us so badly.

On Dec. 23, the well guy told us he'd be here the next day to put his equipment back together and start drilling. That morning, Christmas Eve, he called. His wife had been in a car accident, and he was on his way to the hospital.

Get a lawyer, someone advised us. Sue him. Get his equipment towed out of there. Kick the guy while he's down.

But we hung in there with him. Partly because we'd made a deal. He wasn't holding us to it anymore, said he wouldn't blame us for hiring someone else. We did, in mid-November, call another driller, but he had jobs lined up for weeks.

And we hung in there because we hoped he'd give us a really good deal, maybe just charge us for materials. All this suffering would be worth it when we got the bill for a mere two thousand bucks.

Just after New Year's, the other guy called and said he could drill our well the Monday after next. On Jan. 15, water ran through the pipes in our house. I laughed and screamed when I turned on the kitchen faucet, and the water streamed out and down the drain. My daughter cried.

So what was the lesson in all this? I don't know. But I do know that having water is worth whatever we have to pay for it.

Honor Thy Father...

Dear Dad.

Thanks for all you've done and all you still do.

Happy Fathers Day.

Gee, the greeting on that card sounds so nice. But what if "all" Dad did was not so great?

What kind of Father's Day card do you buy for the grandfather who sexually molests his little grandson? Or the father who left his (wife and) children to start another family elsewhere? Or the dad who spends his paycheck on whiskey?

Do we pretend everything's OK on Father's Day? For the sake of keeping peace in the family? So we don't hurt anyone's feelings? So we don't disrupt anyone's concept of reality?

For Jews, Christians and Muslims, paying respect to Dad is not an option—it's a command: "Honor your father...so that you may enjoy long life...."

When I was little, Dad was my Prince Charming. He was generous, funny and popular. He adored me, bought me lots of gifts, told me how pretty I was and was convinced of my great intelligence, talent and poise.

After he died 10 years ago, a chain of events—a downward spiral of events—made me realize—no, smacked me in the face with the fact that Dad was no Prince Charming. It's not that I learned any dark secrets: I just saw what was there all the time. I had believed a self-protective myth for 35 years. This myth put all the blame on Mom for the problems in our family. If she wasn't so depressed, so religious, so critical, life would have been OK, I thought.

The truth is, they were both screwed up. Perhaps I played make-believe all those years, afraid the truth would destroy me. It didn't. It set me free. That is, after the anger subsided, after the grieving was done, after acceptance settled in.

When I was "in denial," believing Dad was Prince Charming, it was like the truth was locked in a room inside me. A room I could not enter, but a part of me nonetheless. I was destined, doomed, to live it out. I thought and felt things I could not understand, was locked into committing acts against my will.

We see this in families where child abuse or alcoholism seems to be a hereditary trait passed down through the generations. Growing up, the children in these families hate what's going on, yet, as adults, find themselves committing the same sins.

We were not allowed to tell anyone what actually went on inside the four walls of our home. We were not allowed to tell anyone that Mom smacked us around and screamed at us. We were not allowed to tell anyone that Dad beat up on Mom. We were not allowed to tell anyone that Dad came home late, drunk, regularly.

We were a nice family. Nice nice nice.

Discovering the truth shocked me. Angered me. Then I grieved the loss of the wonderful childhood that never really was. (There were wonderful things about it, just not in the ways I pretended.) Talking with relatives, I found out stuff about my dad's childhood that didn't fit in to the rosy picture of bygone days. It did not absolve him of his sinful choices, but it helped me understand him.

When I forgave him, I was freed (not magically all at once) of his sins, no longer doomed to live them out—in one form or other—and pass them on to another generation.

Now I see my Dad as a whole real person, not a myth. He was funny and fearsome, generous and abusive, popular and troubled. A human being trying to make sense of life. During the last few years before he died, he called often just to tell me he loved me.

I honor him.

Lift Up Your Eyes

"It must have been an unusually clear and beautiful night for someone to have said, 'Let's wake the baby and show her the stars,'" writes Madeleine L'Engle in *The Irrational Season*.

At 3:30 a.m. Sunday the pitter-patter of big feet awakens me from a light sleep. My eldest child (she's 26) is walking around downstairs, having come from her home in Staunton to watch the meteor shower.

After a cup of hot tea, Heidi, the husband and I drive to the back-field. Leaning against the Land Rover, we just begin to enjoy the Leonid meteor show when our necks inform us they'll soon be sore. So the husband goes to fetch the flatbed truck, complete with futon mattress, a wide sleeping bag for cover and pillows.

There we lay with our first born, warmed between us in the cold night. Light streaks appear and disappear above and all around us.

Of course it is beautiful.

This stargazing is part of our family history. Out in Jollett Hollow, where we lived for 13 years, the night sky was blackest black. We spent many nights lying atop sleeping bags on our hillside deck, staring into deep space at the moon and stars and planets. Those memories are more precious to me than any obligatory treks to King's Dominion.

> *Because of the light of the moon,*
> *Silver is found on the moor;*
> *And because of the light of the sun,*
> *There is gold on the walls of the poor.*
> *Because of the light of the stars,*
> *Planets are found in the stream*
> *And because of the light of your eyes,*
> *There is love in the depths of my dream.*
>
> —"Alchemy" by Francis Carlin

L'Engle continues, "The night sky,...the stupendous light of the stars, all made an indelible impression on me."

As in the past, on Sunday morning we sometimes point, chat and laugh. "Look," I point out, and "ooh."

"My eyes were closed because I was yawning," says Heidi.

"My eyes were crossed because I was farting," says the husband.

At other times we are silent together. Looking. Being. The vastness of the universe again strikes me. So much out there, so infinite.

"I was intuitively aware not only of a beauty I had never seen before but also that the world was far greater than the protected limits of the small child's world which was all that I had known thus far," writes L'Engle.

While I'm driving to work or loading the dishwasher or watching a movie, so much is going on out there. Meteorites colliding, old stars crumbling, galaxies forming, planets turning, moons reflecting, comets swooshing trails of dust.

This summer the husband and I drove out to the Stokesville Observatory. Through the lens of a powerful telescope, I saw a spiral galaxy thousands of light-years away. What I was seeing was actually centuries ago because of the time it takes light to travel, the amateur astronomer told me.

And at Green Bank Observatory in West Virginia, through the largest moveable radio telescope in the world, scientists listen to sounds from the edge of the known universe. Sounds made hundreds of thousands of years ago.

There is so much I do not know. I am privileged to be a part of this immense universe, just as I am an intimate part of these two people here with me. And in the merciless passage of centuries past and future, here I am. My obligation to live out my purpose in this place and time is just as real as my responsibility to these two loved ones.

How can I not take that seriously? How can I ever become complacent? How can I ever think I know it all, that I even know much?

Lift up your eyes and look to the heavens:
Who created all these?
He who brings out the starry host one by one,
and calls them each by name.
Because of his great power and mighty strength,
not one of them is missing.

—Isaiah 40:26

When light begins to creep up from the horizon, we three return to the warm house, bringing with us a memory and changed by our shared experience.

Of Humans and Being

o o o o o o o o o o o o o o o o o o o o o o o o o o o o o o o o

"We care what happens to people only in proportion as we know what people are."

—*Henry James*

An Unexpected Death

I knew her for only four days, 17 years ago.

Why do I care so much that she's gone?

I met Becky Evans in May 1982 at a convention in Atlanta. She drove there alone from Jackson Hole, Wyoming. With little money, she could not afford a room and was sleeping in her car in the Omni parking lot. That didn't seem to bother her.

I visited her car one day and it did look as though she was living in it.

A tough-looking small woman. About 4 foot 10, muscular. Short sandy hair and freckles. Gentle. Easy laugh.

It was one of those rare meetings, for me anyway. I take months to warm to people. But every once in a while, I meet someone with whom I instantly bond. Becky was one of those people.

My husband and I offered to share meals with her in our room, and we offered our shower. She took us up on it.

I remember little of what we talked about, all these years later. She was a truck driver and had some stories to tell about that, one in which she almost died in a blizzard driving in the Rocky Mountains. As we got better acquainted in those few days, she shared some of the hard, personal stuff of her life, a very different life than my own. She was living on the winning side.

After we returned home, the letters began. She called me Nancy because she said I reminded her of someone. She even addressed her letters to Nancy Austin.

She wrote long—10 to 12 pages—letters in tiny script. A lot about the woods and mountains and plants and animals found in the Yellowstone National Park. Her home—Jackson Hole—was (is) an entrance to the park. She spent a lot of time trekking around the park, as I did the Shenandoah National Park.

She taught me to identify and track animals, not by their footprints, but by a more sure method: their feces. I laughed, but it worked.

She called God "Sir."

The letters came often for the first few years. Then dwindled to a few a year, then we corresponded only at Christmas, then it was just a card. Signed, Becky.

My kids knew Becky vicariously. When they were young and being educated at home, I read her letters aloud to them. She was Mom's friend Becky in Wyoming. Of course, we were all going to go out there someday, to see Becky and visit Yellowstone.

This past December, when I was sending Christmas cards, I came upon her address in my book, as usual. I hadn't received a card from her in 1997.

Should I send her one? I wondered. Why am I keeping in touch with this woman I don't really know?

I sent it.

One day last week, when I got the mail out of the box, there was a letter in the pile with a return address from a Virginia Evans in Riverton, Wyoming.

Oh no. No.

There was a letter. And this photocopy: "Evans, Rebecca S., 49, Riverton, Wyoming. Passed away Jan. 10, 1999 in Denver, Colorado, of Ruptured Brain Aneurysm and Stroke.…"

Mrs. Evan's letter was written with the same tiny scrawl and eloquence as her daughter's. She and Becky had been returning from Dallas, Texas, in November when Becky had a seizure. Mrs. Evans sat by her daughter's bedside for 45 days in Denver while Becky was in a coma. Becky regained consciousness for about a week before she suffered a stroke and died.

"She was as sweet as ever and never complained," wrote Mrs. Evans. "Jesus was still her best friend, a sweeter Christian I have never known."

Becky had been on dialysis—she had complete kidney failure—for two years. Which explains why, perhaps, she hadn't sent me a card in 1997. However, she was well enough last summer to buy herself a "huge" 25-year-old Harley-Davidson.

When her mother chided her for it, Becky replied, "Yes, Mom, but I've always wanted one and since I can't work, I can look at it every day and maybe someday I will be strong enough to ride it."

Gosh how I cried last week when I read that letter. I wonder why I care so much about a woman I hardly knew. But as long as she was alive, she was out there, out in Wyoming somewhere, my friend Becky in Wyoming.

And now she's not.

Dear Dad: If You Could See Me Now

Dad often told me (and anyone else who would listen) as I was growing up that I was going to be the first female president of the United States.

Such was the expectation I had to live up to.

My first mistake was learning to ride a bicycle when I was 4. My grandfather had given me an adult-size bicycle. I couldn't even sit on the seat, but after more than a few bumps and bruises, I cruised on down the sidewalk.

"Look, Daddy, see what I can do," I yelled.

From my first straight-A report card in first grade, Dad was convinced I was a prodigy. Making good grades was as effortless as stepping on an ant, so I didn't have to try too hard for Dad's approval. He gave me enough dollars for each A to start a small savings account.

When I was 8, he bought me a plastic organ, and immediately I was propelled to the status of budding musician. Guests in our home were subjected to my labored recitals of "Row, Row, Row Your Boat" and "Mary Had A Little Lamb," while Dad gloated.

When I began studying French in seventh grade, Dad bought me a subscription to Quinto Lingo magazine. He kept me regularly supplied with reading material that was way over my head.

In the meantime, he began grooming me for my political career. When I was old enough, he took me to rallies and campaign events. He aspired to and ran for local offices himself, but never won an election.

The campaign trail was fun. Once, as someone's campaign manager, he got a long flatbed truck with side racks and had a band play on the back of it. There were lots of other people on it, too, including me. We cruised from shopping plaza to shopping plaza, singing and clapping. Mostly we sang "You Are My Sunshine." Then Dad would make a speech and the guy we were campaigning for (darned if I remember who or what he was running for) made a speech.

There was a basic difference between me and Dad. He was great at starting things (for example, over a 20-year period he owned three restaurants that went bankrupt) but not so great at seeing them through.

He watched me learn to water-ski on (well, I was more in than on) Maine's Casco Bay when I was 12. I pulled up on the skis for a few seconds, then plunged into the frigid water, time after time, for hours.

When I returned to the dock, exhausted, he said, "Why did you keep getting back up again?" He didn't understand my tenacity.

My life did not turn out the way Dad planned it. I married young instead of going to college, had children instead of a career and moved to a remote hollow in the mountains of Virginia instead of an upper-crust suburb of New York.

Each of the three times I told him I was pregnant, he said, "Oh, my God." When he first visited my home in the hollow, with all our chickens, cows, goats and pigs, he said, "I've wanted to do a lot of things in my life, but this was never one of them."

I thought Dad would be excited when I served as a delegate to the Virginia Republican convention a few years back, but he wasn't real happy about it. His Connecticut license plates said "DEMOCRAT."

He was proud, though, when I wrote for a small newspaper more than 10 years ago. It was a shoddy paper at the time, and my writing was awful. He kept asking me to send him clippings with my byline, and I didn't. I knew he would show off the articles to his friends, who would be just as impressed with my writing as our guests had been with my organ-playing sessions.

But I really impressed him when, at 35, I ran the Marine Corps Marathon. He ordered pictures of me crossing the finish and displayed one in his living room. What impressed him most was the endurance it took to train (for six months) up to the 26.2 miler.

"How could you do that?" he asked.

When he died in 1991 it was a strange but real comfort that I'd finally won his approval at something.

My stepmother told me later he'd finally conceded that, in spite of my disparate lifestyle, I just might be happy.

I miss Dad most at times when I've accomplished something. When I won the first-place award for column writing from the Virginia Press Association in February, he was the one I ached to tell. Kind of a look-Daddy-see-what-I-can-do type of thing.

Will I ever outgrow that?

Moving Around The Court

It's like I'm standing in my junior high school gym playing volleyball and a voice from behind me booms, "Rotate!" As we shuffle around the S, a girl on the front line steps off the court and a new player joins the back line.

I heard that voice the other day.

My parents moved a lot when I was a kid, every couple of years. Though I missed my old friends, I always made new ones—one best friend and a smattering of playmates. That pattern, of changing friends every few years, has continued into my adult life.

As I make ready for the next shuffle, I've been thinking about those friends. Some of them, especially up through my teenage years, were pretty shallow. We didn't share secrets or discuss anything meaningful. We shopped, partied, got into trouble, got out of trouble, double-dated, talked about clothes and boys and other girls.

Then I had a few young mother friends. We were friends because we were young and we were mothers. Secretly, I got so sick of prattling about diaper brands and Junior's doctor visits and late-night feedings that I stopped answering the phone and even hid a few times when one came to the door. At social gatherings, I avoided the kitchen with lines like, "Oh, I'll just get in your way," preferring the company of men.

Then I met Toni. My first "kindred spirit" friend. The first time she came to my house, we stayed up until dawn talking. We told each other things we'd never told anyone, giggled, cried…. We felt we'd always known each other. We felt understood.

I don't know about other people, but this way of knowing someone happens to me rarely. Just a few times in my life.

Along with Toni came the rest of the Cannazons. She had five sisters and a brother. My home became a "safe house" for her sister, Patty, when she was being abused by her husband. One night she showed up on my doorstep wrapped in a towel, a baby on each hip. Then her sister Annie moved in to help take care of the babies. There was nothing Toni and I wouldn't do for each other.

After a few years, Toni moved to Florida, then I to Virginia. We wrote, phoned and visited. Even after many years, Toni said to me, "I have never found another friend like you." But I lost touch with her a few years ago when she and her husband separated. I don't know where she is.

In the meantime, I've had some good, close friends. I'm not the type to have lots of friends, just a few. I've had several chance encounters with people I feel "kindred" with. It always takes me by surprise, always exhilarates me.

Four years ago I met Peggy at a meeting I was covering for the newspaper. Our kinship was instant. People at the meeting who observed us talking thought we'd known each other for years.

Peggy came into my life at a critical time. We were both at a point, in our late 30's, when we were taking honest, hard looks at our selves—where we were, what we were, and why we were who we were.

This was serious stuff and we spent hours and hours talking and listening, helping each other find our way, and laughing. Laughter is one of Peggy's gifts. When I shared the most awful, horrible, low-down things about myself, she would laugh. And then I would see how funny it was and laugh—rolling, bellyache, eye-tearing laughter.

When I get down on myself, which I often do, Peggy shows me qualities and virtues—worth—I am reluctant to see I have. And she doesn't do it in a now-I'm-putting-on-my-encouragement hat kind of way. She really believes it. She knows the worst of me, yet believes the best.

Now Peggy has graduated and is moving back to Boston and getting married. I am happy for her, though I shall miss her terribly. She will always be my friend, just as Toni is still my friend. I am grateful for these precious friendships. It seems I'm not meant to keep them with me.

When I heard that voice a few days ago boom, "Rotate," I knew that though Peggy was stepping off the court, she will still be cheering me on. And I wonder who will appear on the back line.

The English Teacher

It was an innocent enough assignment: Write in a journal every day. Hand it in on Fridays, get it back each Monday.

So I wrote. I wrote about my neighbors, school, books, the Vietnam war, music, my backyard. My first entry on Sept. 15, 1969, says: "Although I won't be able to write any personal experiences, it'll be nice to look at this when I'm older." It is nice.

Here are a few lines from Oct. 14: "There's going to be a Peace March from our school in Patchogue down to the bay in Bellport. There's going to be guitar playing and singing, speeches, discussions...Whenever I think of a Peace March, I think of what I see on TV, with police all over the place."

When I received my journal Monday mornings, I always leafed through the most recent entries to check Mr. Hughes' comments. Often it was just a scribbled "Good."

Before many weeks had passed, though, I had become comfortable with my pen and my rust-colored composition book, and with Mr. Hughes' weekly inspection. On Oct. 20, 1969 I wrote: "I think I'm making this journal too personal for a teacher to read..." In the margin Mr. Hughes scribbled "I don't mind."

At 15, I hated the war and the "Establishment" with the rest of my generation, but struggled with where I fit in: "However much hippies search for peace in the world, they will not find it. It is destined to worsen. The only peace we will ever find is within ourselves, with God...Peace—what is it? Do you stand up and yell for it? Do you kill for it? I do not know Peace yet."

I was also preoccupied with pollution: "Try to find one clean spot with no filth, grease, factory waste, paper, beer cans, untread before by 'civilized' people..."

To add to my confusion about the world and my adolescent identity crisis, my parents were separating and getting divorced that year. Nov. 3: "I tried to talk to my mother and we had a fight. I tried to tell her why I resented her. It's probably because in the middle of the best summer of my whole life, she decided she was getting a divorce and took me and my brother and sisters to my grandmother's house…In that month, my mother tried to get me on her side, against my father. On a weekend visiting my father, he cried to me of how he needed us and how I could stop this whole business. I did my best to cover up my feelings about everything and nobody thought I was affected by it at all. They said I hadn't any feelings. But I was being pulled at from both sides and was very hurt…"

I wrote corny pain-filled poetry, for which Mr. Hughes gave me high grades, just for making the attempt. He wrote "Yay!" after this one: "Millions of promises, Made and broken, A word of apology, Phony, if spoken."

As I scan through that 27-year-old journal now, I notice he always gave me low scores for superficial teacher-pleasing entries, and high grades and more comments when I spilled my guts. "You express yourself well," "Keep writing," "You write very well."

On April 8, 1970, I finally responded: "Thank you very much for encouraging me to write. I feel now as if I have something more to live for. I love to just sit down and write."

Then I read through a classmate's journal. Each entry was pages long, with lavish handwriting and flowery adjectives. On May 7, I wrote to Mr. Hughes: "Could you please tell me how to improve my writing? I just read Mona Simon's journal and was very, very impressed. I think I am too frank and to the point when I write." He had his wife, a published writer, respond. She said, "Good God! Never be anything but frank. A writer provides a point of view against which we can measure our own. Clarity, simplicity of expression and directness are each a part of good writing…Never apologize in writing…just plunge ahead and say it…You write well, think well, and it's a lifetime endeavor, you know. Learning goes on and on…"

That helped. A professional writer was giving me affirmation. That day, I began to identify myself as a writer.

When the school year ended I continued to chronicle the divorce of my parents, pen poems and songs, unleash my anger at people and institutions, play with sounds and senses of words, pour out my grief, describe glorious and dreary spring and autumn days…

I think back about that period of my life, when the world and my world were falling apart, and Mr. Hughes (I don't even know his first name or remember what he looks like) seems to have been placed there by providence. He never judged me, always understood, always encouraged. I trusted him.

An Unforgettable Valentine

Since this is Valentine's Day I thought I'd write about a real Valentine—Valentine DeCarlo, my 8th grade English teacher.

Mr. DeCarlo looked and "tawked" like Joe Pesci. He was a short, funny man with that distinctive accent of a refined New York Italian. He had Pesci's dark, thinning hair and big nose. He wore the type of eyeglasses that are supposed to slide to the end of your nose, giving him the appearance of being intellectual—which, to my young, impressionable mind, he proved to be.

I don't know how he could afford these on a teacher's salary, but Mr. DeCarlo wore at least three or four big (and I mean *big*) multiple-diamond rings, which overpowered his pudgy fingers. The biggest one was on his pinky. The third period sunlight pouring through the windows set his rings a-dazzle, and, since he couldn't talk without ardent hand gestures (and he talked constantly), we were further dazzled by the prisms of light shooting about the walls of the otherwise dismal classroom.

One of the strangest things about Mr. DeCarlo was his suits. They were of fine fabrics, cuffed, always well pressed and in various shades of gray. But they were too big for him, purposely. I assume it was purposely because I can't imagine him not doing it on purpose. His cuffs dragged on the floor. His sleeves came almost to the tops of his fingers. The shoulders hung down. The crotch flapped around between his legs and the jacket extended to his mid-thighs.

To complete the ensemble, Mr. DeCarlo wore obviously well-made brightly polished black shoes. With taps. Yes, I said with taps. And since he couldn't talk without strutting around the room, the taps kept constant, regular rhythm to his ongoing soliloquy. I always wondered—did the shoe store install the taps for him? Did he have a custom shoemaker who built the taps into the shoes? Or did Mr. DeCarlo have an inventory of taps in a closet at home and hammer them in himself?

But these questions, and the one about, "Why do you wear your suits so big?" I kept to myself. They were not the sort of questions you asked Mr. DeCarlo, even when he was in a joking around mood.

Even if Mr. DeCarlo hadn't had these idiosyncrasies, he still would've dazzled us. For, in contrast to the dull teachers who droned and drilled dryly, Mr. DeCarlo was as interesting as his demeanor. And he made us think.

As he walked and talked and gesticulated, our eyes followed him, down the aisle, up the aisle, across the front of the room and down another aisle, riveted by his commanding voice. Maybe the taps helped. He was absorbed in his train of thought, skillful at the articulation of those thoughts, drawing us into his thoughts. To divert a group of adolescents caught in the throes of puberty from our preoccupation with the opposite sex, acne and hairdos was no small feat.

Mr. DeCarlo could point out a word or a sentence, nuances in whatever the poem, story or essay, and with it, question the very foundation of the world. He never asked the standard comprehension or vocabulary questions. He assumed we comprehended elementary things like the sequence of events, plot and setting. What he questioned was motives, beliefs, why the author used certain words and turns of phrase, and, getting down to the marrow of all good literature, the meaning of life and of death.

It's almost as if he, a teacher, actually (gasp!) respected us—13-and 14-year-olds.

There were no glib explanations here, nor any glib answers. Better to say, "I don't know, Mr. DeCarlo," than spit out a pat reply. I remember him talking about reincarnation, strutting up and down the aisles, taps tapping, hands waving. Suddenly he stopped—a dramatic effect (we were always aware that we were watching a showman of sorts)—right next to my desk, and, bending down to me, peering out from over the glasses and from under his bushy black eyebrows, asked, "Brown (he called us all by our last names), what did I mean by that last statement?"

I did not then nor do I now believe in reincarnation, and I don't know that he did either, but I appreciate that he respected me enough to let me reach that conclusion myself. He taught me that doubt and questioning are not to be feared—although I didn't understand that then.

"There lives more faith in honest doubt, Believe me, than in half the creeds," wrote Tennyson.

I enjoy being challenged, intellectually, on what I believe. Mr. DeCarlo's motives were not to convince us of a point of view or to ridicule. That is rare. If he had, I would have withdrawn or put my dukes up.

I am reluctant to argue, but, if pressed, can answer somewhat reasonably about things I'm sure of. And the only things I'm sure of are what I've thought long and hard about, struggled with, anguished over, tested, because they've been challenged previously by doubt—either from another person, my own conscience or by life's jolting disruptions.

Those disruptive doubts are scary, the kind that pester me—suggesting that I'm not as honest, or loyal, or kind, or generous as I like to think I am; that I don't practice what I preach; that my motives for doing good may be self-serving

"Doubts are messengers of the Living One to the honest," said Victorian writer George MacDonald. "They are the first knock at our door of things that are not yet, but have to be, understood...Doubt must precede every deeper assurance; for uncertainties are what we first see when we look into regions hitherto unknown, unexplored, unannexed."

Mr. DeCarlo—rings, taps and all—defied definition, and definitions.

I've never known another Valentine.

Are You Being Helped?

OK, OK, here's a test.

1. You started running a few months ago and now you want to run in a 5K race. Who do you ask for advice?

    a. your 300 lb. couch potato brother who knows everything

    b. a co-worker who has run 5K's and longer races

    c. a friend who tried running a few times

2. You decide to prepare your first eye of round roast for your family. Where do you look for help?

    a. The Betty Crocker Cookbook

    b. a friend whose roasts are grey and dry

    c. your horoscope

It doesn't take a doctorate in philosophy to figure out the best choices, yet in real life, people often look for advice in all the wrong places.

I was inspired by the story of Liza Vann, a woman who was diagnosed with breast cancer and 10 years later still has both breasts intact. The producer of a film about Vann told me that Vann got little support from support groups.

Support groups, she found, can be a great source of comfort and strength if you make the same decisions they made. Vann found when she decided to pursue the least damaging method of ridding her body of cancer, she was bucking the system. She was on her own.

When I decided to run a marathon in 1989 I decided to run a marathon. I did not decide to "try" to run a marathon. I decided to do it. There's a big difference.

After making this decision, I did not listen to the advice of the obese woman who watched me run by her front porch each morning.

"My chiropractor says you'll get back problems from running," she said.

I read the marathon training program in Runner's World magazine, over and over and over. I indoctrinated myself with that program. And I talked with the few people I knew who had run marathons. People who knew from experience that completing a marathon is possible.

"I'll try," is OK when you're tasting plantains for the first time or buying new shoes, but not when you're planning a marathon or other important goal. Because when the situation gets impossible—the thighs turn to concrete, the company does not hire you, the row of stitches is on the wrong side—you, my friend, will give up. Throw in the towel.

Marriage is not a place for "trying" either.

In the midst of a marital difficulty, a thrice-divorced woman advised me, "Give it your best shot," swigging a gulp of Michelob Light and puffing on a Marlboro. I had not asked for her advice, nor would it have occurred to me to do so.

These "sadder-but-wiser" types offer advice most freely, but not to help you succeed and share your happiness. When you make the same choices they have made, it justifies their failure and keeps their "I'm a victim" identity intact.

The people we ask for help don't have to be perfect, but we should respect the way they handle their struggles. Commiserating and escaping has its place, but not in healing.

As I heard a preacher once say, "Hurt people hurt people. Healed people heal people." It is out of those healed places inside us that we can touch others.

On the Internet, I came across this gem on *Dean's home page*:

"Your must constantly ask yourself these questions: 'Who am I around? What are they doing to me? What have they got me reading? What have they got me saying? Where do they have me going? What do they have me thinking?'

"And most important: 'What do they have me becoming?'

"Then ask yourself the big question: 'Is it OK?'"

Find someone who has done what you want to do. Read good books. Read the Bible. Learn to rely on God, whose mercy endures forever, believes the best of you and who will never, ever give up on you.

Christmas

o o o o o o o o o o o o o o o o o o o o o o o o o o o o o o o o

"Our house is open, Lord, to thee,
Come in and share our Christmas tree!"

—*Lucy Shaw*

It is a Most Holy Night

It was a few days before Easter when I realized there was no such person as Santa Claus.

My second-grade classmates had made fun of me that day for the stupidity of believing there was an Easter Bunny. I ambled home with my eyes on the sidewalk, not even stopping to watch the ducks on Corey Creek.

"Mom!" I shouted when I walked in the door. "Mom!"

Mom appeared at the archway into the living room.

"There's no such thing as the Easter Bunny, is there, Mom?" She hesitated, then shook her head. "No, honey," she said.

And that's when it hit me. "That means there's no such thing as Santa Claus either," I said.

Mom made no reply.

No Easter Bunny I could handle. But no Santa Claus? No Santa Claus? I felt like I'd been had.

Would Christmas be empty without Santa Claus? Maybe not.

The Christmas following that revelation, I kept my grown-up secret from my younger brother and sisters—why spoil it for them? After they'd gone to bed, Dad took me to my Aunt Joyce's house, a few blocks away. He, my grandfather and I sat on the couches in front of the fireplace.

I remember the crackling and warmth of the fire, the scented candle burning on the coffee table and the sound of their hushed voices, talking into the night. It was one of those rare occasions when time seems suspended and all is well with the world.

Christmas Eve was, is, still magical.

There was the warm Christmas Eve that Kim (my husband) came home just after noon with a round bale from Ray Comer's. When he tried to drive up the hill to the house, the bale fell off, bursting its cords as it hit the ground. The whole family, adults and little ones, spent the rest of the afternoon scooping up great armfuls of the hay, still fresh with the smell of summer fields, and throwing it back on the truck.

Sometimes little Rachel picked up so much we couldn't see her as she carried it to the truck bed.

When we finally got most of it off the ground, Kim drove the load across the pasture to the barn. Daniel and I climbed onto the truck bed and pushed the hay off in huge heaps, and when we pushed the last heap, we fell into the manger on top of it, laughing all the way. Then everyone else jumped in.

There was the much colder Christmas Eve, when our friends the Clarks came over. A few inches of snow were frozen to the ground from a snowfall a few weeks earlier. We shared a candlelight meal at the table in the great room, close to the wood stove.

After dinner we made candles and ornaments with the beeswax, wicks and forms Melissa had brought from home. The children enjoyed this, proud of their creations, and then they went sleigh riding. The green floodlight was on outside and they spent hours whizzing down the slick driveway and tugging the sleds back up. Every so often a child would come in, red-faced with cold and excitement, to warm up with a cup of hot chocolate, and dash right out again.

Rachel remembers this as her favorite Christmas Eve—one she would like to live again.

What is it that transforms these ordinary events into something magical and memorable? Is "the true meaning of Christmas" really definable, solid, able to be grasped and held?

Can anyone explain how God came to earth as the man Jesus, as one of us; surrounded by, as Walt Whitman says, "beautiful, curious, breathing, laughing (and I would add sweating, whining, sickly) flesh?" It is a bit far-fetched. Can anyone understand how each of us is created in his image…making every birth, every life, an incarnation?

To me, it is a mystery. And I find I must salvage my childhood imagination, my childhood faith and the "love I seemed to lose with my lost saints"—Santa Claus, Mom and Dad, and all the others through my life up until yesterday who disappointed me—to believe it.

The wise men brought gifts to the child Jesus, Immanuel—God with us—and we, in turn, bring gifts to each other.

There is a doctrine that says God created man because he was lonely and wanted fellowship. Bah, Humbug! Would that not make God selfish and needy, a codependent kinda guy? It is simply a case of man making God in his image.

God is love, and the first thing I see him doing is creating—earth, sun, moon, stars, trees, birds, animals—and he saw that it was good. Then he made man and woman, patterned after himself, to give it to.

I see God incarnate in my husband as he works in the garden, in my daughter Heidi when she paints still-lifes, in my friend Margie as she arranges dried flower bouquets, in my mother-in-law as she puts dinner on the table. I see the creator in my editor (though he would deny any resemblance) when he explodes through the newsroom door in the morning and rustles open the paper to look at the page he created the day before. And he sees that is good.

I see God in my family as we create the Christmas tree—an icon—and in the faces of people—who seem happier at Christmas, when they are being generous.

"The fullness of joy is to behold God in everything," said Lady Julian of Norwich.

As the sun sets on Christmas Eve the children start saying, "Light the candles, Mom, let's turn out the lights."

And so we light the bayberry candles. The multi-colored lights strung on the beam overhead faintly illuminate the transparent paper angels hanging there. The tree-and bell-shaped cookies, the cheeses and crackers, the eggnog, the breads and wine are brought and placed on the red and gold cloth-covered coffee table. The Christmas songs—*Away In A Manger* and *Silent Night*—play softly on the stereo or I play them on my guitar.

In this gentle light we gather. I look at the radiant eyes, the contented smiles, of the ones I love. To be here together is enough. Even our laughter seems hushed, hallowed.

As *Star Trek*'s Dr. Spock would say, "It is not logical." But no matter.

It is a most holy night.

The Case of the Christmas Tree

As Christmas draws near, images of intimate family scenes come to mind: baking cookies together, making decorations, putting up the tree, eating and drinking with much laughter and goodwill.

One of the regional differences between "up North" and here in the Valley is when people put up their Christmas tree. I had lived here just a few months when the holiday season came. I was already trying to adjust to being called "ma'am" at the tender age of 23, to afternoon being called "evening," to thinking of Harrisonburg as a "city" (in contrast to New York City), and a host of other cultural incongruities. But when I observed my neighbors putting up their Christmas trees on Thanksgiving weekend, I was aghast.

I have a friend in another county who puts up her tree at Thanksgiving. Then, on Christmas morning, as soon as the last package is opened, she takes it down. She is so sick of it by then.

For many Northern folks, putting up the tree is a Christmas Eve activity. From what I remember, most do it up within a week before Christmas. Some take it down just before New Year's Eve, some after.

I don't like waiting until Christmas Eve. Even though, every year, my husband says we always put it up on Christmas Eve. But we don't. Maybe a few times. We usually put it up about a week before.

We've always had a real tree. Artificial trees are so predictable. You know what kind it will be and what shape, that you won't have to trim it if it's too high, that if you forget to water it, it won't turn brown. Natural trees, besides the fact that they're real and smells and all, are not predictable. Each one has its own character.

The first year my husband and I were married, back in the 70s, we had a psychedelic tree, complete with homemade day-glow decorations. The four-foot blacklight, on the floor behind it, set the scene aglow. Not exactly homey but, hey, we were still hippies.

When we moved to the hollow in Elkton, we sold Christmas trees. The hill on our seven-acre tract was crowded with cedar and pines, just the right size. We needed to clear the land anyway, so we cut them and took them into town. Got five bucks apiece for them. It was great being able to step out the back door and cut down a tree.

After some years went by the pines got too big to use for Christmas. One year, I had just read a poignant little story to my youngest daughter about a poor family that was so grateful for their hemlock Christmas tree. With the tears still wet in our eyes, we set out in the snow to find a hemlock.

After traipsing around awhile, we found one, densely crowded in with others. With my dull axe, I chopped and chopped until it came down. Away from its siblings, the hemlock was scanty-looking. What could we do? With a flash of ingenuity, I decided to cut another one, wire them together and…ta-da…a full tree. We dragged them into the house, bound them together, and put them in the stand.

Hmm. Still scanty. Another flash.

We went back out, this time with a hacksaw, and cut branches off hemlocks. Then we attached them to the tree with twisties. It still looked rather ill. When everyone else came home, I attempted to create the sentimental illusion of the poor family with the hemlock tree, but I still suffered much ridicule over that sad tree. Especially when, after a few days, the pseudo-branches turned brown.

Then there is the annual Tinsel War. I wonder if there have been any divorces over tinsel? I can see the couple now, standing before the judge, and he asks: "What are the grounds for this divorce?"

The wife says quietly, "It was the tinsel, sir."

"The tinsel?" the judge asks.

"Yes," she says, starting to cry. "He hurls globs of tinsel at our beautiful Christmas tree. He's such a brute. I cannot live with a man like that."

The husband says, "She would rather take six hours to place one strand of tinsel at the very tip of each branch."

"At least you can still see the tree when I'm done," she screams at him.

The gavel strikes. "Divorce granted, next case."

A Christmas Rose

Christmas can be difficult for families split by separation and divorce. This holiday, like no other, is about having our loved ones around us.

Where to go at Christmas was not an issue when my parents divorced. My mother, a Jehovah's Witness, did not believe in Christmas. While my parents were married she had done Christmas with us anyway, trying, I suppose, to keep the peace.

So when Dad remarried, there was no squabble about where the kids would go for Christmas. It was off to Dad and Rosanne's. For me, at 16, adjusting to the divorce and remarriage was tough, but the transition to Christmas with Dad and Rosanne was not.

Rosanne was 26 when she became stepmother to me and my siblings, ages 10-16. She was much different from my mom.

She had short hair, big glasses and big earrings. Being a schoolteacher, and being Rosanne, she had an air of authority about her. She was sometimes loud and always cheerful—laughter bubbled from somewhere inside her and made her eyes and whole face sparkle.

She was also warm and interested in us kids. It did not take us long to love her. I called her my friendmother.

Rosanne loved Christmas. She decorated the apartment in early December with things she made herself. She wore red and green sweaters, poinsettia earrings, Christmas tree pins…if it had to do with Christmas, she had it and she did it.

She made Christmas goodies I'd never seen before—candy cane cookies, merry cheese squares, jam thumbprints, cheese balls. The stuff was stashed everywhere in Tupperware containers. And she sewed Christmas stockings for us kids, something we'd never had.

Rosanne shopped for Christmas year-round. Even on summer vacation. I could tell the gifts she bought from the ones Dad bought. One year Dad bought me the D-Day album, a two-record narrative of the invasion of Normandy. Yeah. A few years later she bought me all the Beatles' albums recorded to date.

She had every Christmas album ever recorded. She stacked the records on the turntable and played them continuously—Nat King Cole, Jose Feliciano, the Chipmunks. The one that epitomizes her is the Supremes, with Diana Ross belting out "Santa Claus is coming to town."

Rosanne's family, the McKaharays, were Irish Catholic. They accepted us kids into their family as their own. Grandma McKaharay made Chex mix every year and sent it in gift-wrapped coffee cans to everyone in the family. That and fruitcake. When she passed away, I began (and continue) to make the Chex mix and my father made the fruitcakes.

I'll never forget that first Christmas at Dad and Rosanne's. It was a tradition for Dad to make a huge delicious breakfast of sausage, bacon, scrambled eggs and lots of other stuff. And he always bought a stollen at the bakery in Bellport. That year our breakfast also included Grandma McKaharay's rum cake, which we liked so much we ate lots of it. When we stood up after breakfast, we fell back into our chairs again.

Later, after Christmas dinner, Rosanne made me help clean up. This may seem natural, but for years I had evaded doing dishes after holiday dinners by excusing myself right after dessert to go to the bathroom. There I stayed for a half-hour. Rosanne caught onto this real quick, and came banging on the bathroom door.

"Come out of there, Luanne," she hollered. "You're not going to hide in there while your sisters and I do all work." She was laughing. And I laughed, too, emerging sheep-faced.

So at age 16, my idea of Christmas changed. Not all are blessed to have a stepmother like Rosanne. My Christmas now—decorating, baking, music, candles—reflects her influence.

Rosanne also infected her sixth-grade students with her love for Christmas. After she died in 1993 at age 47, her students planted her favorite Christmas tree, a Scotch pine, in front of Newtown Middle School in Connecticut.

They decorate it every year in her honor.

A Cheesy Christmas Miracle

This is a Christmas miracle. It is a true story.

It starts many years ago, way back in the 1970s. The husband, then 23, began doing tree trimming and removal in order to get firewood to burn and sell. This is how we made the money to move from New York to Virginia.

In the summer of 1978, he did a tree removal job for a German family named Jarvis in Middle Island. Every day at noon, Mrs. Jarvis cooked a great meal. Roast beef, ham, gravy, all the trimmings. While my husband was there working he was invited to eat with the couple.

When he came home at night, he would tell me about what a great cook Mrs. Jarvis was. He was still full from the delicious rich dinner she'd served him at noontime. Even now, all these years later, this woman is a legend in our house.

At the end of the week he came home talking about the fantastic cheesecake he'd had for dessert that day. Not only was it the best cheesecake he'd ever eaten, but Mrs. Jarvis had offered him a choice of fresh fruit toppings. Strawberries, blueberries or cherries.

My husband secured the recipe from her and we brought it with us when we migrated south in September.

We were very poor when we first moved here, so I couldn't even afford to make the recipe. But on our second Christmas here, we decided to splurge on the ingredients for this cheesecake. I borrowed a springform pan and made the cake.

It was very good. But somehow over the years, I lost the recipe.

Although since that time I've made a quick version of cheesecake that's pretty good, it's not real cheesecake baked in a springform pan. And it's certainly nothing like Mrs. Jarvis's.

So a few days ago the husband and I are shopping at the Corning store at the Waynesboro shopping outlet, and we spot these springform pans on sale. So we buy them. And I start hunting for a cheesecake recipe.

Now, I've got 20 cookbooks, so I figure there must be a recipe in one of them that resembles Mrs. Jarvis's. I check first *the New York Times Cookbook*. There are five cheesecake recipes in there, but none like Mrs. Jarvis's. (Even after all these years, I remember a certain ingredient in Mrs. Jarvis's recipe because I've never seen another like it).

The *Favorite Recipes of America* has seven cheesecake recipes. The *American Heritage Cookbook* has one. I check the *Better Homes and Gardens* and *More-With-Less* cookbooks. Nope.

Even the recipe in *Culinary Chefs of Virginia* is rather ordinary. All the recipes I find have cream cheese, of course, and some have sour cream.

So I open *A Quilter's Christmas Cookbook*, with submissions from women who make quilts. In the index, I find eight cheesecake recipes. I turn to the pages and skim the recipes for the by-now-most-highly-prized ingredient.

Nope. None. Then I flip back a page and see a recipe I missed. Hmm. Scanning down the ingredient list, I spot it: 1 lb. ricotta cheese.

Wow! Yay! Yippee! Finally.

Check this out. It also has two eight-ounce packages of cream cheese, a pint of sour cream and a stick of butter. Wow. This stuff is illegal in some places.

I check the name of the recipe. It's just called Cheese Cake.

Under that is the name of the woman who submitted the recipe. My eyes pop out of my head. Oh wow, I don't believe it. It can't be. It's uncanny. Unbelievable. No. Yes.

Eileen Jarvis.

Season Wrapped In Hope

CHRISTMAS (Christ's Mass), annual Christian festival observed on Dec. 25 in the Western Churches to commemorate the birth of Jesus Christ. It is a public holiday in Christian countries, usually marked by the exchange of gifts—tokens of the gifts of the three wise men to the infant Jesus.

Jesus Christ. Christmas is about Jesus Christ.

Offensive, isn't it? It's so offensive, coming right out and saying it like that.

Season's Greetings. Happy Holidays.

There. That's better. A fuzzy greeting that includes everybody. After all, Christmas means different things to different people.

Having grown up with Christmas without Christ, the holiday to me meant the closeness of family, the goodwill of mankind and friends, and lots of food and gifts.

No matter what Mom and Dad were going through—financially or marriagely—they always managed to make Christmas special for us kids. Until they divorced, of course. Then, emotionally, we all went our separate ways.

For children in safe, happy places, Christmas is a time of magic and love. But for many it means Mom or Dad getting drunk and getting nasty and fighting. Some children look out the window for a Dad who never shows up.

Mankind? Weeks ago, my car dealer let me not pay for a part not covered under my warranty because I told him we had to drill a new well. Sometimes people let me ahead of them in line at the grocery store. Our first Christmas in Virginia we were broke, and a neighbor brought us bags of groceries. A woman at the beach saved my daughter from drowning at age 4.

Mankind also cuts me off on the highway and yells at me for existing. Mankind raped and killed my friend Susan Dranitzke and Debbie O'Rourke's little sister, Alice. Mankind shot three students praying at school a few weeks ago. Mankind regularly exterminates whole groups of peoples.

The goodies? Fruitcake and sugar cookies, nuts and fruits, cheeses and egg nog and spiced cider. The foods of Christmas are definitely part of holiday. And, in January, they are definitely part of me. So I either stay away from the goodies or feel guilty about eating them.

If I'm depending on my good family or mankind's goodwill or goodies to give me that warm holiday feeling, well, hey: sometimes it happens, and sometimes it doesn't.

This year is the first I've been aware of Advent, the four Sundays before Christmas when we anticipate Christ's coming. Like Mary, I am waiting, pregnant with hope.

I cry as I sing the carols about the Redeemer's birth and the joy of his coming. I think it is because life—everyone's, and mine in particular—makes no sense without redemption.

"For there is no doubt at all that there does persist the feeling, and it is probably the deepest one we have, that what matters most is that we learn through living."—Doris Lessing, *Summer Before the Dark.*

I tell people, in the way of comfort, that nothing is beyond Christ's redemption. It sounds so feeble a thing to say sometimes. Yet this knowing was hard-won—learned the hard way, if you will—and I bear the scars.

The only way to know about redemption is to need it. And then to have to wait for it.

Even in my own circle of acquaintances, I ask: Can he redeem the death of my friends' 30-year-old daughter, a wife and mother of two? Can he redeem the cancer of a 17-year-old baseball-playing teen? Can he redeem the wounds inflicted on a middle-aged couple by the leaders of their church? Can he redeem a marriage that is all but dead? Can he redeem the sexual abuse of a young girl?

"God did not abolish the fact of evil: He transformed it. He did not stop the crucifixion: He rose from the dead."—Dorothy Sayers, *Mind of the Maker.*

"Let every heart prepare him room." If we would experience his redemption, we must make a place for him. Hope does that. An atom of hope in a heart full of doubt, mistrust, cynicism, despair…but hope nonetheless.

Even the Bible says we must be fools to believe in him.

So either have a generic happy holiday with fully functional happy families, faith in mankind's goodness and gaily-wrapped consumer goods, or celebrate Christmas.

This year I am waiting for Christ.

Are You Ready For Christmas?

"Are you ready for Christmas?"

This question is asked of me, but I do not ask it. What does it mean: "Are you ready?" In what way? How does one prepare for Christmas?

If you mean in the American consumery kind of way, then, no, I am not ready for Christmas. I've done little shopping. A few things here and there, and those mostly from small shops and artisans.

Do I get points for visiting the Mall for the first time in a year, even if I bought nothing?

What I wanted to do was make (sew, crochet, bake) gifts, but as a working-outside-the-home person, this is an absurd aspiration. Let the time that is past suffice for thoughtful, handmade gifts.

Am I ready for Christmas? I've done absolutely no baking. Not a cookie, nor a loaf of bread nor a sweet.

When I was a full-time homemaker, I began baking Dec. 1, carefully storing the goodies in airtight containers. Lots of kinds of cookies: Mexican wedding cakes, chocolate chip, peanut butter, shaped sugar cookies, chocolate peanut butter chip. I baked egg nog poppy seed bread, banana bread and pumpkin bread, as well as stollen and coffee cakes.

Mostly, I no longer bake mass quantities for self-preservation. Not only did I do most of the baking, but also most of the eating. Then I spent the rest of the winter dieting to get the extra 10-15 pounds off.

I don't think so.

Working-outside-the-home mothers who do bake 90 dozen cookies, hand-make their Christmas decorations, help with the class party and buy gifts for even the mail man...all while keeping their homes immaculate and hosting and attending lovely dinner parties...must be frenzied and frazzled. At least that's what I tell myself. I can't do it. I don't.

As for decorating, I've got a couple of pine cones in a basket and some lights out front. We're picking up a tree today.

Growing up, "up North," most folks put up the tree on Christmas Eve. When I moved to Virginia, I compromised by putting up the tree the weekend before Christmas. Since most people around here buy their trees at or shortly after Thanksgiving, by the time we get there, there are just a few scraggly trees are left to choose from.

The perfect Christmas tree is so elusive. Perhaps the first ones, the ones that Martin Luther saw when he gazed up and saw the stars shining through the tall pines in his yard, were the very best.

That I have been doing. During my morning run and going places in the car, I've been gazing at the glory. Yesterday when my husband was driving, seeing me turn in my seat to look at the purple mountains' majesty against the spacious sky, he asked, "Have you ever been out before?"

And I have been reading Bible passages foretelling the birth of Christ, and about the birth of John the Baptist, and about the angel coming to Mary and then to Joseph. I've been thinking about the mystery. You know, about God coming to live among us.

It would be like wanting to help a people group, like say Palestinians on the West Bank or Latinos in a ghetto or child prostitutes in Bangkok, but you can't because you're not one of them so you arrange to be born among them but still with a higher perspective and telling them about it and then maybe one day in a street fight sacrificing yourself to save their lives.

I've been thinking about the mystery, the big plan, God's unfailing love. His mercies new every day.

And thinking about Jesus, prophesied as the Prince of Peace and where is the peace? Is it in us, among us? If so, how do we share it? How does it spread?

Like Mary, the mother of Jesus, I ponder these things in my heart. God knew she (and humankind) was ready, even while she was asking the angel, "How can this be?"

Yes (gulp), I am ready for Christmas.

Things We Have Passed

How many loved your moments of glad grace,
And loved your beauty with love false or true,
But one man loved the pilgrim soul in you,
And loved the sorrows of your changing face...

—William Butler Yeats

Thinking It Through

It is early. Out the window over my desk, I watch the cattle graze in the pasture. In the winter, they scavenge for the hard brown grass, even when it's poking through crusted snow.

Later, they will bring the grass back up from their storage stomachs (rumen) and chew it. They stand immobile when they do this, their jaws barely moving. Ruminating. That's what they do. They chew it slowly, over a period of hours, until it's fine enough to digest.

> *"In our sleep, pain that cannot forget falls drop by drop upon the heart and in our own despair, against our will, comes wisdom by the awful grace of God."*
>
> —Aeschylus

Dreaming, thinking, listening, being still…it's all ruminating. The coarse, undigested stuff of life comes up from its storage place when it is ready. While we sleep, our minds are quiet, freeing the imagination to filter through the facts of our lives.

Even when we don't remember our dreams, our imaginations are still doing the work of sifting through the events, facts, and feelings of our days. I like what Thomas Moore says about dreams in *Care of the Soul*, that we do not interpret our dreams—they interpret us.

Imagination numbs us from feeling the pain in our lives or invigorates all our senses. We use our imaginations when we're in denial. To make believe, in the face of hard facts, that a problem does not exist, takes a lot of work on the part of our imaginations—whether it's justifying destructive behavior, faulting others for our failures or pretending everything was grand.

I do not like feeling raw, vulnerable to life's elements. Those who have lost their childlike ability to imagine need help to numb the pain—alcohol, food, spending money, religion, a sports car, other people's problems—anything that can be obsessed about.

Cattle would not grow if they thought of the coarse grass, "I can't handle this," and refuse to eat it; or spit it out once they found it was too hard too chew; or keep it repressed in their storage stomachs. Neither do we grow when we refuse to eat that which life sets before us, that which appears unpalatable.

The same imagination that enables us to deny engages us in hope. To hope when there is no hope, our imaginations must find a grain on which to nibble, to ruminate. And with each thought, each dream, each talk with a friend, each small act of belief, what we hope for comes that much closer to our grasp.

In its raw state, grief is indigestible. When a death or tragedy first occurs, the real stuff of it gets stored away. Then, over time, it comes up to be broken down into digestible substance—as tears, memories, confusion, anger, conflict, remorse, honesty, laughter, truth.

Regret, shame and guilt are indigestible. Those things that, when recalled, drive us crazy, that are hard to even think about. No amount of psychological analysis or justification or excuses can wipe it away.

Over time, drop by tiny drop, wisdom comes: Because of who I was then, it could not have been any other way.

If I am alive, I cannot avoid pain. Some people's lives are so filled with pain, it doesn't seem fair. Yet many refuse to be bitter, refuse to become the "living dead," instead letting their pain be redeemed.

> *Imagination, which, in truth,*
> *Is but another name for absolute power*
> *And clearest insight, amplitude of mind,*
> *And Reason in her most exalted Mood.*

—William Wordsworth

Meditating on and imagining truth can lead us anywhere. Who would have thought man would walk on the moon? Who would have thought we could converse with someone in China? Yet mankind, through the centuries, walked toward its own unbelievable possibilities.

So it is with each life.

It starts with ruminating, thinking slowly and deeply on that which is set before us—the dry coarse stuff as well as the delicious—then imagining that raw material into whatever shapes we desire, and making our life with it.

That 'Justahousewife' Makes Her Smile

"And what do you do? Are you justahousewife?"

The used car salesman needed to know my occupation to process our loan. I looked at him with a half-smile.

"Yes, justahousewife," I said.

As the salesman's pen touched the paper, my husband leaned closer to see what he was writing.

"Make sure you write it like that—'justahousewife,'" my husband told him.

The salesman smiled tentatively at what he thought was a joke, and began writing. My husband stopped him.

"Justahousewife starts with a 'J'. Write justahousewife."

After a few more times of this, the salesman realized he was serious (kind of), and wrote "justahousewife" in the blank, but not without subjecting me to a condescending little speech. You know, the one that starts off with, "Well, that's a full time job in itself…"

I was amused.

These days, justahousewives are women who make conscious decisions to stay home to care for their families full time. Women's "liberation" has made it unpopular. Children's author Madeleine L'Engle reported that she was inundated with angry letters when her *A Wrinkle In Time* heroine, Meg, decided to stay home to raise a family (she eventually had five children) after graduating college. I think Meg was gutsy.

When I decided to be justahousewife, I was also deciding not to have a lot of stuff. Rather than money, I invested time into my children.

Instead of vacations to Disneyworld, we hiked in the mountains identifying birds and wildflowers and catching lizards. Instead of treats at ice cream shops, my kids ate oat and honey bread, still warm from the wood cookstove. Instead of viewing *Teenage Mutant Ninja Turtles* at the theater, we snuggled up and read about Toad's adventures in *Wind in the Willows*. Instead of sitting on the couch gazing at a Nintendo screen, the kids created roads and towns for their Matchbox cars in the backyard.

I had a working friend who bragged about spending $35 for a pair of Bugle Boy jeans for her son. At $5 an hour, that means she worked seven hours for them. I bought the same ones for a buck at a yard sale. And how many hours did she have to spend away from her son to buy his $120 sneakers? (I wonder what would happen if American consumers, i.e. suckers, refused to pay that much for a pair of sneakers?)

For some reason (I'll let you guess), my presence often elicited in some women a need to explain why they had to work. One said she'd go crazy sitting around the house all day doing nothing. She worked in a factory sewing the inseams on jeans all day. Another woman yelled about how she could never center her life around waiting on a man hand and foot and be his doormat and fulfill his every whim. Another, whose income combined with her husband's totaled $80,000, told me they wouldn't "have anything" if she didn't work.

I was amused.

Because of the progress made by women's lib, we are now measured by the same standards as men—in dollars and cents. I struggled often with that imposed pressure.

It was hard being with women who could afford to dress fashionably, get haircuts every six weeks and "do lunch" with their girlfriends. It was hard having friends visit my "handyman special" home with my second-hand furniture and renovations-in-progress. It was hard to say to the kids, "No, we're not going to King's Dominion with the rest of the church."

I had to decide to be a homemaker over and over again, ask myself, "What is important to me?" In spite of the pressure to "be something," to have stuff, I knew I had made the right choice.

Because as a homemaker, I was doing just that—making a home Not just a place where a group of people took showers, slept and grabbed a bite to eat. Not a showcase for our stuff.

Guests often said our home was a peaceful place.

In my free time, I read and wrote. I devoured the poetry of William Blake, T.S. Eliot, Robert Browning; the prose of Charles Dickens, C.S. Lewis, Herman Melville. I read history and science books, the Bible and biographies. I read articles and columns in newspapers.

I wrote letters and essays and poetry. I sat outside and watched cows and wrote about the way they chewed, the way they walked, about the way the wind sounded and felt. I sat in a laundromat and wrote about the way mothers yelled at their children, how men folded their clothes. I wrote in my journal about the things my children said and did, about my parents and my childhood, about God and marriage and life.

You see, all the years of being justahousewife, I was also a writer. And I knew that someday, someone would pay me to write. I did not feel deprived or anxious about it. I just knew. There is a time and season for all things.

The only place I wanted to work was at the Daily News-Record.

For now, this time and season, while my kids are teenagers, I work part-time. I am not willing to give up sewing dresses for my daughters, baking an occasional loaf of bread, eating dinner together each night.

And so now, when someone asks me what I do, I say I am a newspaper reporter and columnist. That impresses them.

And I am still amused.

Is Happy the Norm?

Warm days and blue skies and daffodils.

Who could not be drawn out-of-doors by the loveliness of recent days? After all the grayness and rain, the spring weather has been impossible to resist.

Are days like this the normal state of things? When my son Daniel was little, on rainy days he would say, "It's a beautiful day." After many times I began to wonder, what beauty does he see in this rainy day?

I went into a church years ago feeling down and the congregation was singing a bouncy song: "Never never never have I ever ever ever been so happy happy happy with my Lord...."

The pace and mood of the singing was frantic—at least it felt so in my despondency. Rather than being caught up in their enthusiasm, I felt I was in a group of happiholics. ("We must be happy. We must stay happy.") I'm sure many of them were happy, but out of a hundred people, chances are they didn't all feel that way. Yes, yes, yes, I know God gives us a deep abiding joy and we sing these songs often "by faith," but I'm not talking about that.

I'm talking about this perception we have that our normal state of being is happy and fulfilled. Is there something dreadfully wrong with us if we're not, as Felix Unger sang to Oscar Madison, "Happy and peppy and bursting with love?"

There is another song—written by Pete Seeger—that speaks to me much more really: "To everything—turn, turn, turn—There is a season—turn, turn, turn—And a time for every purpose under heaven. A time to be born, a time to die; A time to plant, a time to reap; A time to kill, a time to heal; A time to laugh, a time to weep."

I don't like that part about "a time to kill, a time to heal." Is there any "purpose under heaven" in killing? I want to blot that out. Yet killing happens. It happens. It's reality.

I am trying to understand a grief I've been carrying. Grief for what? A lot of things all at once. Things I don't normally let myself dwell on. Losses of all different kinds: people I love who have died, my youth, my children's childhoods, old friends. Other people's losses. The way of the world—pollution, gross immorality, materialism. All the things I can do nothing about.

I'm a non-cryer, yet I've teared up and cried at the most surprising times lately: in the shower, on the motorcycle, waking up in the night.

My first reaction to this ache-in-my-gut feeling was that something is wrong and I must identify it, analyze it and fix it. And then I read the passage in Ecclesiastes from which *Turn, Turn, Turn* is taken. I decided to hang in there with the grief and see where it takes me.

Perhaps this is my time to weep.

Fortunately I have wonderful friends and family. Wonderful because they're getting the brunt of my negativity. Wonderful because they're helping me in my grief—not trying to get me through it or over it or away from it—but staying with me in it.

It's like when someone dies and we ask about the surviving spouse or child, "How is she doing?" In America, if they're crying and upset and hysterical we hear they are not doing well. If they're keeping their chin up and all that we hear they are bearing up pretty well.

And a few days ago I read this passage in *The Rosemary Tree* by Elizabeth Goudge:

"You know, Miss Giles, you're all wrong about yourself. People who have lost the power of love don't grieve over its apparent loss. They don't grieve over anything. If you've lost the power of love you've lost the power of grief. Hold on and the tide will turn."

"Hold on to what?" asked Miss Giles.

"To grief," said John.

Miss Giles was silent. "I've never done that," she said at last. "I mean, I've never welcomed anything difficult or painful. I've always resented it and hit back. I can see now that to have welcomed the slings and arrows might have been to welcome love."

"There's never any 'might have been' with those who retain the power of grief and the power of tenacity," said John.

I don't like feeling like this. But I hope the author of this book and of Ecclesiastes know what they're talking about. I hope to be able to hang in there with it long enough to come out the other side. I hope there is another side to come out of.

And to see the beauty of a rainy day.

How We Seem To Others, Ourselves

Some time ago I received a letter from a reader expressing her admiration for my writing. She also wrote, "You seem like a well-adjusted career woman, Christian, wife and mother."

"Ha," I said, showing the lines to my editor. "Look, Joe. I'm actually pulling this off. I'm fooling them."

What we seem to others and what we seem to ourselves to be is often very different. The key word here is "seem."

As for being a good writer, perhaps that is true. But the truth beneath that is that I struggle with it continually. I am not consistently a good writer. My early training in writing was my journals, into which I bled the joys and, more often, the pain of my life. And it seems I write best when I'm opening a vein to let my heart pump the words out.

That's scary. And I'm not just saying that. It's not something I'm willing to do often for the public. My best writing is stuffed in the closets or under the beds of my friends, and only my closest ones at that.

But occasionally, as C.S. Lewis writes in his preface to *Surprised by Joy*, "I have been emboldened to write of it because I notice that a man seldom mentions what he had supposed to be his most idiosyncratic sensations without receiving from at least one (often more) of those present the reply, 'What! Have you felt that way too? I always thought I was the only one.'"

And, from the inside looking out, I'm not a well adjusted anything.

Yes, people may see me attired in a blazer and skirt carrying my little briefcase. But I never feel any mastery over my "career." I conduct every interview and write every story with trepidation: Have I asked the right questions? Am I leaving something important out? Do I really understand what I'm writing about? Am I representing this person or situation or issue accurately and fairly? Am I bringing too much of my own bias to this story?

Assailed with these doubts, I manage (usually) to pull it off.

Doubts are a bigger problem when it comes to being a Christian. The reader called me a Christian, a designation I don't think I've ever claimed in my columns. In the New Testament book of Acts, it says the followers of Christ were first called Christians by the residents of Antioch. "Little Christs," it means.

Hey, I live inside here with my doubts and my flailing about and my prejudices and my selfishness and my hypocrisy and my ulterior motives. And I live more by hope than faith. If others call me a Christian, a "little Christ," I hope it's because of what I am and not because I can quote Bible verses. I don't think I'm much like Jesus Christ, not by a long shot.

As for the wife and mother part…close relationships like that are all about learning to love. I don't think it's something any of us ever get a handle on. An act of love that gives help one day may be a hindrance the next. (My kids are growing up now: At what point does my providing food, shelter and cash become harmful to their maturing?) How is one to know the difference? What we do not know by intuition or wisdom we must learn, alas, by making mistakes, by hindsight.

My best friends tell me, "You're too hard on yourself." They (thank God for them) believe of me better than I believe of myself. "Love allows a person to see the true angelic nature of another person, the halo, the aureole of divinity," writes Thomas Moore in *Care of the Soul*. That's why we need friends, need the little notes, the hugs, the look-you-square-in-the-eye raps about how great we are.

In *Pilgrim's Inn* by Elizabeth Goudge, a friend tells a friend, "This sense of futility…it's nothing, merely the reverse side of aspiration, and inevitable, just as failure is inevitable. Disregard them both. What can we expect when we aspire as we do yet remain what we are?"

I don't expect perfection of myself (or do I?), but I do expect progress. I want to be better today than I was yesterday.

"What we are is nothing; what we seek is everything," said Friedrich Holderlin. Maybe that's what my friends see. If that is true, I guess I'm OK.

The Invisible Girl

Looking across the train car, I saw my reflection in the window opposite, for by now it was dark outside. My coat's golden fur-lined hood was draped over my shoulders. The chestnut suede coat transformed me from the ordinary Luanne Brown into a beautiful and sophisticated young woman. But then I wasn't wearing my glasses, so I couldn't see the frizz radiating from my unruly blonde hair or the ever-present pimples on my adolescent face.

Someone else on that train, however, was more worthy of my attention. He was the prince of my dreams, the sum of all the heroes in all the gothic romances I had ever read. Tall and slender, with wavy, brunette hair and a "classic" nose, he stood out against the bland background of medium-height, medium-hair, medium-featured boys. He was Richard.

Yet to him, seated by the aforementioned window, I was invisible. He messed around with his buddies, throwing things, yelling dares and wrestling. A teacher admonished him sternly, threatening to never bring him on another field trip and what a disgrace he was to his school. His only response was a smile.

And then it happened. The moment I remember on that 8th-grade field trip to Philadelphia better than any other. The Liberty Bell, Independence Hall and Betsy Ross pale in comparison to that moment.

Richard suddenly stood, crossed the aisle, and, leaning over, handed me a Baby Ruth candy bar. Oh, oh, oh!

"Thank you," I stammered. My timid, mud-colored eyes stared into his sparkling, thickly-lashed ones. He turned, went back to his seat and his friends, and I was invisible again. During the two years of junior high school, that was the only time Richard ever acknowledged my existence.

I became invisible the day I entered kindergarten.

My first day at Blue Point Elementary School, the clinically sweet teachers were impressed with my ability to print my name. Obviously, it didn't take much to impress them.

The oldest of four children, I was in charge at home and in my neighborhood. But stuck in an institution with its artificial expectations, rules and regulations, and particular hierarchies, I became shy and withdrawn. I did what was expected of me, made consistent A's on report cards and did nothing to get noticed.

When I did speak, it seemed nobody heard me, like I wasn't even there.

In 7th grade—junior high—I befriended other friendless girls: Norma, a Puerto Rican with whom the American girls felt uncomfortable; Susan, a Jew whom the other Jewish girls accused of being a lesbian; and Barbara, a big-mouthed gawk who was always putting her foot in her mouth.

We were a little band of rejects. Boys did not ask us to go steady or to dance or go out. We had fun. Goofy stupid we-don't-have-to-try-to-be-cute fun.

We had each other.

In high school our clique broke up, dispersed to the uttermost regions of the larger institution.

Not everyone's school experience was like mine. Perhaps some actually thrive in that environment. I appeared to. Some of us jump through the hoops with one hand behind our backs, while our real selves shrivel or find life elsewhere.

As an adult, my relationship to institutions—denominations, corporations, government agencies—has not changed. It is why I rail against the Glom and conformity to popular culture.

To the U.S. government, I am a taxpayer, a number. At Wal-Mart, I am a consumer. At large gatherings, I am a wallflower.

It has taken many years to find an identity apart from how I am defined by collective and powerful people. It started when I met my Creator, who has filled me with confidence and strength.

Even so, at mid-life, this feeling of being invisible returns in odd moments to haunt me.

I cling to these lines from a poem by Robert Browning:

> *All, I could never be,*
> *All, men ignored in me,*
> *This, I was worth to God...*

Encounter with the Past

I saw her at the grocery store last week. (Remember, remember).

She's not anyone you would notice. She leaned on her cart on the cereal aisle in a sweatshirt and jeans, talking to another shopper. I heard her say that her husband gave her $60 to shop with. That was supposed to feed them and their two kids for a week.

She reminded me of another woman, a woman I knew long ago.

This woman, as carefully as she tabulated, often had at the checkout more groceries than money. So she had to decide what to put back. The oatmeal or the tea? The kids need the oatmeal but I can live without tea, she thought.

She arrived home to a hungry baby and a sink full of dishes. First feed the baby while watching a *Star Trek* rerun. The dishes, well to be honest, they were there this morning and as a matter of fact they were last night's dishes. She'd wash them as dinner cooked.

In the bathroom, she noticed again the roots of her Sun-In bleached hair were dark, matching the mascara smudged under her eyes. At 22, she felt fat and ugly, though she weighed only two pounds over what it said on the Metropolitan Life Insurance chart and she had an attractive face.

Her only new clothes these days were hand-me-downs from her younger sister who attended college. She couldn't imagine spending any money on a new blouse or even a pair of jeans for herself.

The baby cried. She cursed, thinking, "Can't I have just a minute to myself?" and left her image in the bathroom mirror to see what was wrong. He'd wriggled his lower half under the couch and was stuck. He looked so funny with his little red face that she laughed as she bent to pull him out.

Later, she settled down with a paperback, a nondescript romance. Anything to distract her. Even so, after a few minutes her mind began to wander from the paragraphs. She thought that someday she'd like to write professionally. But.

The "but" was she rarely finished anything she started. How could she expect to finish writing a book? Or even an essay? Out in the yard was an antique medicine cabinet she'd started refinishing. Over by the sewing machine was a few swatches of a bed-sized quilt.

Another "but" was she didn't know enough about anything to write about. Expelled from one high school, she barely scraped through the classes at another to get a diploma. Not that she wasn't smart enough. But she had cut classes and gotten suspended four times in her senior year, almost getting expelled again.

Then, at 19, she got married and started having babies.

Spiraling down through her failures and faults, she began to feel hungry. Ice cream. No, there was none. How about cereal—there's plenty of that. So she did. Three bowls.

Her husband's return gave her someone to pour out her frustrations on, her bitterness. In the bedroom, she complained about not having enough money for groceries, about the landlord, about the lack of heat in the apartment.

He didn't have to be told that they didn't have enough money or that the apartment was cold. He felt she was blaming him, that it was his fault; if he was a better man he'd be providing better. He yelled at her to shut up, just shut up and get away from me.

Retreating to the couch, she began to cry, a rare (not even annual) event for her. I am so stupid and so horrible, she thought. How can I ever change?

As she sat there, into her mind came a picture, a picture of her but a much different her, a better her. She was wearing white and her face glowed with serenity and virtue, intelligence and confidence. And she was loved...so so loved.

That few-second image changed her forever. It replaced the one in the bathroom mirror. It replaced the one she saw reflected in the faces of the people around her, past, present and future.

It was instantaneous, yet has been, still is, a journey.

I saw her at the grocery store last week. I wanted to give her some cash, but I had none in my wallet, just a dollar or two. More than that, I could have given her this:

All, I could never be,
All, men ignored in me,
This, I was worth to God.

—Robert Browning

September

The blooms of the thistles on the roadsides have turned deep brown, like cigar stubs.

The tall green stalks of summer have dried beige and crispy. So plenteous and prosperous has been the corn this summer. Some fields are being cut now, sheer down to the ground, leaving behind little but a chance crackly stalk or ear.

Do gleaners come along and pick up the corn that's left?

Great flocks of swallows swarm from fences to branches to electrical wires. Flying overhead, their multitudes look like vast dark clouds, darkening the sky. So distinct and delicate each one is. From below each one looks like a small jet.

Crows, brash and bullying, descend in swarms too, into the pines of the woods across the street. Dressed in black, they are like a roaming gang, looking for trouble. In the mornings, they are like the neighborhood alarm clock, just as insistent, yet somehow much more pleasant.

In turn, my running over the old iron bridge at 7 a.m. rouses the ducks resting on the girders beneath. Quacking, cackling and fussing, they descend and, with no time to consult, scatter up and down the river, skimming the water's surface.

Only the leaves on the swamp maples along the river's edge have started to yellow and brown, as have those on the tulip tree outside my kitchen sink window.

It is so loud at night, with crickets and hordes of unknown, unseen insects chirping, cheeping, squeaking, shrilling. The noisiness comes from high in the oak and maple trees, from the woods across the street, from the bushes around the house.

And the air, "this nipping air, Sent from some distant clime where Winter wields His icy scimitar, a foretaste yields Of bitter change…," (W. Wordsworth) is no longer of the sultry heated variety. It is drier, clearer, cooler, joyous.

With each leaf that goldens, each swallow that takes flight each ear that is harvested, we move closer to…what. September is the beginning, the beginning of the end, and the end. No longer summer, not yet autumn.

> *Oh, then I knew at last that my own autumn was upon me,*
> *I felt it in my blood,*
> *Restless as dwindling streams that still remember*
> *The music of their flood.*
>
> —Sarah Teasdale

At 46-almost-47, I am between seasons. Not yet autumn, definitely not spring. The heat of summer is past, yet the restlessness remains, the wanting.

> *The year might age, and cloudy*
> *The lessening day might close,*
> *But air of other summers*
> *Breathed from beyond the snows,*
> *And I had hope of those.*
> *They came and were and are not*
> *And come no more anew...*
>
> —A.E. Houseman

In September, we say to each other, "Gee, is summer gone already?" And I wonder: do people say that in nursing homes?

I go to work, to school. From where I sit inside the windows that are never opened ever in a climate-controlled environment, the clear sky and waving treetops call. "It's too nice to stay inside," I hear my mother say.

I want to say, "Can we open the windows? Can we at least hear the blue jays, the jets, the shouting? Can we at least feel the warm cool-nipped breeze? Can we at least see the sky and an occasional bird fly by? Can we at least smell the fresh-cut grain or even the fumes of passing traffic?"

There is still so much to enjoy, to love, to know. Winter will be here all too soon.

What Color Is The Sunset?

Oct. 25, 1998: There is no name for the color of the sunset tonight.

Perhaps that's as it should be. Some things are beyond our ability to peg, tag, name and number. And yet we try to describe it, to hold it in our minds in some categorized way so that we can understand it, grasp it, to bring it into subjection to human reasoning.

I could say the clouds are a pinkish gray. Or grayish pink, shot with streaks of light. To the east they are herringbone-shaped, spotted against the baby blue sky. Moving west the clouds get wispy, as though the artist barely touched the canvas with the swirl of his paintbrush.

In my small corner of the world tonight, I hear a neighbor's rooster crow, a garage door closing, the lowing of a herd of cattle.

As I scribble these words, and the sun drops lower, night chill also descends. I go into the house for a sweater, and whisper the word "sylvanshine" to my husband at the keyboard. I saw that word the other day and he reminds me that it's a Tolkien word.

Sylvanshine is the moonlight that shines through the woods and into my bedroom window. It's the rich golden light that fills my yard when the sun shines through the yellow and copper leaves of the maple tree. Like alchemy, turning everything to gold.

All is transformed at this moment. I think I must go in to start dinner but I do not move. As the sun nears the horizon, it shines up to underneath the clouds, deepening the pink against the shadows above. What color is that? I ask.

I sit here on the hard, cold bucket of the tractor in the twilight because of yesterday. Because the beauty of a few moments yesterday have made me greedy for beauty today.

It ravished me yesterday, in a moment I will remember all my life. Like the time I came face to face with a deer in the woods at the Sportsmen's Club in Oakdale. Like sitting on the bow of the motorboat chopping through the waves on Casco Bay.

Like that, but more.

I was motorcycling down a stretch of road in West Virginia in mid-afternoon Saturday. This road—W.Va. 220—cuts in the hollow between mountains north to south. The hills gave us great bouquets of color all afternoon.

Then we—our group of motorcyclists—came round a bend to another world. To my left, a rounded single mountain rose sheer above a river. The sunlight shone onto the mountainside at an angle from behind me, illuminating the golds and maroons. Cropped bright grass lined the road's edge, sloping gently down an expanse of field to the river.

My words are inadequate for physical description.

It was more than the color. It took me. Possessed me.

It invaded my vision, rushed through my head and infused all my senses. And I ached for it, to be part of it, to give myself to it, to its is-ness.

It pulled at something in me, something buried and ineffable.

I wept.

If they had known it was there, they would have charged admission. They would have sold postcards and plastic dyed mountains and Beanie Babies. They would have erected a McDonalds and a Ramada Inn. They would have stamped that square acreage with a UPC number.

They would have come with their cameras to take pictures of their spouses at the edge of the river, would have stood in the field making calls on their cell phones to arrange for next week's support group meeting, would have dropped the white cardboard from their Little Debbies on the grass.

As it was, there was a solitary car in the park.

I remember this as I watch the sun drop behind Shenandoah Mountain to the west tonight. I think of all the sunsets of all the days since the world began. A thousand years ago. The sunset on this day 45 years ago, the day my parents wed. The sunsets watched by other lovers who lived in my house a hundred years ago.

And another day in the long, long story of planet earth is over.

Listening to Winter

Here we feel but the penalty of Adam,
The seasons' difference; as, the icy fang
And churlish chiding of the winter's wind,
Which, when it bites and blows upon my body,
Even till I shrink with cold, I smile and say,
'This is no flattery.'

—from *As You Like It* by William Shakespeare

It is cold. Perhaps not as cold as it could be or should be or would be, but it is cold. The cold permeates everything. Even my house, which is old and drafty. Even me, with my sluggish metabolism.

Where to get warm? Next to a wood stove hot with fire, on the road running, in bed snuggled under quilts; eating hot potato soup, drinking hot chocolate, baking homemade bread.

The visual does not help: Everything is stripped bare, the trees and shrubs, gardens and yards, valley and hills. The insects and birds left in autumn with the last tourist. Gone from our mountains, hotels and restaurants are the hikers, bicyclists and picnickers, the fathers with camcorders and cameras, the young men and women trekking the Appalachian trail, the senior citizens in travel buses. Gone.

We humans have taken extra layers. We bundle up in undershirts, long johns, sweaters, gloves, coats, hats and scarves.

Out my front window, I can see clear through the woods now, rather than to it. In winter, the woods are accessible, free of the undergrowth that hinders my steps in summer. Gone are the violets, trillium and daffodils, the ferns and unknown other greenery.

Gone.

Winter does its best to strip whatever crinkly brown leaves remain on the trees. Pushing with wind, weighing down with heavy snow, wearing out with nightly frost.

Praise the Lord from the earth,…snow and frost,
stormy wind fulfilling his command.

—Psalm 148:8

The frost performs its secret ministry,
Unhelped by any wind.

—Samuel Taylor Coleridge

Shall I struggle against the season? Or shall I, as part of nature, take my cue from it?

The early-setting sun tells me to go home. The cold tells me to stay inside. The bare mountains tell me to simplify, simplify, simplify. The cattle chewing at the brown stubble tell me there's life in the hard ground. The black night sky with its brilliant shining stars tells me to seek only that which is true.

We humans too are regularly stripped of what is hanging on us dead. Clinging to what is past, what was once lovely new growth but now lifeless, makes me a pitiful figure. Green leaves that once took in the sun's light become satiated, grow old and lose their capacity to absorb. They must die and fall away to make way for what comes next.

I do not like winter. I resent the lack of light and warmth. And I do not like facing the icy cold reality of the need to let go, lie dormant, wait in quiet (with questions) for spring. Shakespeare called it "the winter of our discontent."

My instincts tell me to seek after warmth and rest, solitude as well as friendship. I find myself lighting candles for no special occasion but that I need fire.

Rather than trying to escape winter, or merely endure it or gripe about it, perhaps by embracing it I will find something I need and, in my deepest heart, yearn for.

In the bleak midwinter, frosty wind made moan,
Earth stood hard as iron, water like a stone;
Snow had fallen, snow on snow, snow on snow,
In the bleak midwinter, long ago.
Our God, heaven cannot hold him, nor earth sustain;
Heaven and earth shall flee away when he comes to reign.
In the bleak midwinter, a stable place sufficed
The Lord God Almighty, Jesus Christ.

—Christina Rossetti

Am I in Sync?

If we understand the revolutionary transformations caused by new media, we can anticipate and control them; but if we continue in our self-induced subliminal trance, we will be their slaves.

—Marshall McLuhan

Finding Meaning by Context

Context: the parts of a sentence, a paragraph, a discourse, etc. immediately next to or surrounding a specified word or passage and determining its exact meaning; the whole situation, background or environment relevant to a particular event, personality, creation, etc.

We all learned in elementary school to find a word's meaning by its context. In real life, barring a dictionary, a word must often be encountered a few times before its exact meaning can be ascertained.

Determining meaning can be simple when the word is something like "hay," or "bicycle" or "dresser." These words are found in singular settings.

Other words are found in numerous and sometimes unexpected places. Take the word "head," for instance. You can find a head on a person, a glass of beer, a boat, a newspaper, a committee, a tape recorder, a boil, a pin, a peninsula, a sail, a column and a drum.

You can have a head for numbers, head for the bank, keep your head, lose your head, get in over your head, yell your head off, put your heads together and hang your head. To name a few.

In the context of the dictionary, the word "head" has scads of definitions and usages.

Discovering people can be the same way. We get to know most people in particular contexts and ascribe them with a definition. Others, whom we may encounter in a variety of settings, are not so easy to pin down.

And what of our own context? If the meaning of our lives is determined by our context, then what context are we living in? Not long ago I referred to a 16-year-old boy who was a gang member in Los Angeles. When James Langtreaux, a film maker who was doing a video project in the neighborhood, asked the boy how someone can get out of the gang, the boy answered, "You can't."

Is this true? Of course not. From this distance, you and I can clearly see the untruth in which the boy is living. But what would someone say about us?

My husband, who worked for the same company for more than 20 years, could not imagine life without it. He quit a year ago, and life since has been an adventure every day. My brother, told when he was growing up by Dad that he was stupid, could not imagine pursuing higher education. Two years ago, at age 41, he graduated from college. He's living a radically different life now.

"We all live in a context," writes Lynne Bundesen in *One Prayer at a Time*. "The question is, what is that context? Is it theology, biology, an endless round of evil and despair, overworked lives and out-of-reach promises? Or is the context Divine—the essence of Truth. Is it what our poets, prophets and saints have told us, that "in him we live, and move, and have our being?" (Paul: Acts 17:28)

No matter what family I come from, where in the country I live, what my job is, how much I weigh, who likes me, how much money I make, how talented I am, what my theology is or how depressed I may get, the fact of the matter is that in him I live and move and have my being. Period.

It's true for me and it's true for the 16-year-old gang member. It's true for George W. Bush and Bill Clinton. It's true for Timothy McVeigh and Billy Graham.

The question is, are we listening? How conscious are we of Truth?

When pain is assaulting our bodies, when we come from generations of alcoholics, when our jobs drain the life from us, when our spouses leave us, when everyone else seems normal and happy but us…how can we escape our oh-so-defining context?

"Prayer is hearing the Divine Context as if it is our own voice," writes Bundesen.

How do we discern what we're hearing? That's a subject for another time, but one test, writes Bundesen, is to ask yourself: will others benefit?

And in this larger, infinite, loving context, we may find ourselves in unexpected places.

Me and My Buddy, June

"Dear Friend," starts the letter. It's signed "June."

My buddy June is the president of a cosmetics corporation. There's a photograph of her in the left margin—not sitting at a mahogany desk in her navy blue suit, but leaning on a tree in a baggy cotton shirt, her hair slightly tousled. Like we're having this intimate conversation out in the woods.

June is wearing the "Country" makeup collection: Her eyelids are coated with purple eyeshadow, her mouth with magenta lipstick and her cheeks with distinct triangles of rosy blush. The inspiration for this collection, the flyer says, is "a quiet walk in the cool, green woods," and "a bracing splash in a sun-lit pond." I wonder how June's face would look after that bracing splash, with the purple eyeshadow and black mascara streaming down her cheeks.

With these beauty basics comes a "Country" shoulder bag of plastic—oops—I mean "rich tobacco brown leatherette," in which to carry your "essentials."

OK, maybe I'm just enough of a sucker to think buying this makeup will transform me into some sort of wood nymph. That's a common enough ploy. Advertisements often link their products—cars, beer, electronic gadgets, toothpaste—to our egos: our need to feel important, desirable, in control, alive. I have learned to tolerate these insults.

But June has the effrontery to throw in this quote by Henry David Thoreau: "I went to the woods because I wished to live deliberately, to front only the essential facts of life, and see if I could not learn what it had to teach, and not, when I came to die, discover that I had not lived."

Maybe I'm too shallow, but I couldn't make the jump from "essential" beauty products to "essential facts of life." Do people really fall for this stuff?

And those credit card commercials. You know, the ones where they tell you how "in control" you are because you can buy anything you lay your eyes on? Ha! Control is the ability to say no.

Most advertising backfires when it comes to people like me. Then there's peer pressure, which didn't stop after high school.

When I was a full-time homemaker, I didn't have a microwave oven. I had time to make meals from scratch and cook it for as many hours as it took. I did not want a microwave, yet people acted like I was this deprived person in a Third World country because I didn't have one.

Now it's cellular phones. We need cellular phones. Need. To those who still believe you can live without one, I issue this challenge: Will you still think the same way a year from now? Two years from now? As the commercials bombard your mind, as your neighbors, relatives and colleagues begin to use them and consider them as necessary as bathrooms, when people look at you like you're a Neanderthal because you don't have one, will you continue to resist?

Because that's how it feels, once it becomes the norm. Like you're part of some resistance or something.

In *Mind of the Maker*, Dorothy Sayers wrote, "A society in which consumption has to be artificially stimulated in order to keep production going is a society founded on trash and waste, and such a society is a house built on sand."

I wonder when "they" began calling us consumers. Probably when they realized we wouldn't buy all that stuff unless they exploited our most intimate needs: acceptance, respect, love, meaning. They had to de-personalize what they were doing to us.

Let's take Fred Smith, for instance. He was the kid who never made it to second base in Little League, looking up to the bleachers, seeing the disappointment in his father's face, game after game. He was the fellow in high school with all the pimples who could never get a date or speak to any of the popular guys without feeling stupid.

Does Fred Smith feel the acceptance he yearns for in his sleek red sports car? Conspicuously checking his Rolex? In a superficial, sad way, perhaps.

That's what made me mad at June. I take seriously the learning what life has to teach, why I'm here, alive, at this time, in this place. She crossed the line from appealing to vanity, which is the only part of anyone she has any business diddling with, to attempting to exploit a deeply personal need.

I don't think so.

June's mentor, Thoreau, claimed he could buy everything he needed by working six weeks out of the year. I doubt that June's "collection" would have been part of his budget.

Pregnancy: What's A Teen To Do?

"You're pregnant—do you want a termination of pregnancy?"

Doctor Rosenberg asked the question so matter-of-factly, the natural answer seemed to be, "of course." But I didn't say "of course." I told him I needed to think about it.

I never considered that I might be pregnant. This same doctor, president of the Suffolk County Gynecological Association, had told me years ago that I would never have children. When I reminded him of this, he shrugged, saying, "Sorry, I guess I was wrong."

As I rode the congested highway home on my 10-speed bicycle, I thought about it. And I cried. Deep down, I didn't want an abortion. But that's what you did when you were 18 and pregnant on Long Island, N.Y., in 1975. All (yes, all) my friends in high school had had at least one abortion. My best friend, Kathy, had three. Another friend, Barbara, had five, or maybe it was seven. I think she lost count, too.

It was so easy. The Planned Parenthood Clinic in Patchogue gave away abortions like campaign flyers. The yellow pages had scads of abortion clinic ads. Why go through the hassle of using birth control?

Even after marrying and giving birth to two children, Kathy was still haunted by nightmares about the abortions.

When I moved to Virginia, I was struck by the number of teen mothers who lived at home with their parents. I didn't know if they chose to have their babies for moral reasons or because of the lack of free abortion services. I felt rather sorry for the 35-year-old grandmothers who became the martyrs who raised the children. Grandparents are great in their proper roles as grandparents, but generally make lousy surrogate parents.

The director of a local pregnancy agency recently told me that although there is a significant number of teens having abortions in this area, the choice to give birth and keep the child is still typical. She said young teens commonly make comments like, "Oh, my mother will help me take care of it," or "Babies are so cute!" or "All my friends have babies."

One girl told her, "You're considered a nerd if you don't have a baby at football games." Apparently, having a baby gives them a privileged status, like that of owning a Cabbage Patch doll. And unwed motherhood, rather than carrying the stigma it once did, is now glamorized to them by movies and television shows.

In spite of the education and availability about birth control pills and devices, the agency director said girls still see it as a hassle. Some girls keep pills in their school locker, very faithful about taking them Monday through Friday. Devices are viewed as an obstacle to the "spontaneity of the moment."

Although we often hear about the thousands of qualified couples on adoption waiting lists, not many girls are choosing that route. The director said she thinks part of the reason is because we don't see much positive reinforcement of this choice in the media: movies, TV shows, magazine or newspaper articles.

There are no easy answers. Each choice carries its burden of consequences. In my case, my now-husband and I had planned on marriage eventually, and he refused to abort our baby. (What a relief).

My plans for college were scratched. Married during the 70's recession of gas rationing and unemployment, we struggled with (without would be a better word) money problems. Both of us came from dysfunctional homes, and living "happily ever after," I soon discovered, was only in storybooks. And we're still trying to figure out how to be decent parents (we now have three teens: boy, was that doctor wrong).

Sometimes, when I look at my 18-year-old daughter, who has (usually) been such a joy to me, I think back to that awful time of fear and confusion, of having to be grown-up when I wasn't ready for it, of realizing that I was now responsible for another person's life.

I have never regretted my decision not to abort her when she was mere "fetal tissue."

So Much Communication, So Little Access

The world is big and I'm so small
I may as well not be at all.

I scribbled those heartfelt lines at 14, and though I've come a long way since in finding my place in the world, some days I feel like that still.

Like last week when I phoned the Department of Motor Vehicles to discuss a registration mix-up with the office manager, a recorded voice came on the line: "Thank you for calling the Virginia Department of Motor Vehicles. If you are using a touch-tone phone, press 1, if you are using a rotary phone, please stay on the line."

I pressed 1, and a recording gave me a list of options: press 2 for vehicle registration information, press another button for driver's license information and so on, none of which included an offer to talk to the office manager. Feeling flustered, frustrated and futile, I hung up.

Then I thought, this situation does have to do with a registration, maybe I can make some headway there. So I called back and waded through the rigmarole, pressing the appropriate buttons. For registration information I was subjected to a list of basic information about that subject after which I was given the option of speaking with a customer representative.

Is that another term for person? I wondered, and decided to give it a try.

A warm human voice came on the line (yay! Thank you!), giving her name and asking how she could help. I asked for the office manager by name.

"What city is he in?" she asked.

"What do you mean what city?"

"This is the Richmond office."

How the heck did I end up in Richmond? I felt disoriented.

"OK, well, um, Harrisonburg."

"I'll have to call that office and see if he's available and then have him call you back."

What is this guy, the Maharishi or something? Why is this office manager so inaccessible?

He did call back promptly and our business was dispatched quickly and courteously. Now was that so hard?

The same deal happens when I call my doctor. Oops, did I say doctor? I mean, primary health care provider. Who no longer identifies himself by the community in which he practices.

"Hello, this is the Humongous Amalgamated Healthcare Conglomerate. If you'd like an appointment, press 1; if you have a question about billing, press 2; if you'd like to speak with a nurse, press 3..."

Perhaps the next generation won't be so disoriented, so alienated by this. You must remember, the same doctor who delivered me as a baby delivered my dad. When I was a little girl, he came to my house and into my bedroom with his little black bag to examine me when I was sick. Dr. Swenson lived in the big house on Middle Road and went boating with my grandparents.

And, oh, I'm no longer a patient—although it takes a lot of patience (which Ambrose Pierce described as "a minor form of despair") to deal with the Glom. To them, I'm a healthcare consumer. That's a good picture for the dehumanizing, undignified manner in which I'm treated.

However, once I get past the office staff ("And how are we today, Mrs. Austin?"), I like my doctor. When we actually come face-to-face, it is a good, though brief, human encounter.

And then Friday morning I meet with two close friends and we sit and drink coffee and talk about wallpaper, babies, love and marriage, God, me, each of them, exercise, travel, yearnings, coffee, Jesus, women, men, justice...

And that afternoon, when I come home there is a card in the mail for me, from my best friend in Boston. Telling me how wonderful I am and how important our friendship is to her.

In Search Of Something Different

Why must we all look alike?

Some of my valuable time lately has been occupied with one of my least favorite activities: shopping. Not because of Christmas. That kind of shopping is fun.

The kind of shopping I mean is when you go out with a general idea of what you want, only to find, after traipsing from store to store, driving from plaza to plaza, and (later, at home) scrolling through pages and pages of internet sites, that it just does not exist. A 15-minute shop stop turns into hours, days and weeks of searching.

I'm looking for black boots. Black boots dominate shoe store shelves. They have heels, which is why I'm buying them now. Because when heels go back out of style I will not be able to find them for another 20 years within the shores of the United States of America.

But have you noticed that all the black boots look the same?

Oh, the height varies from ankle-to thigh-high. The materials vary from leather to vinyl to fabric. The size of the sole varies, but most have that blobbo platform thing going. I did that already, in the 70s.

I want boots with buckles or laces up the shank, a good pair of boots that will last a few decades. Good shoes can last that long if you get them re-heeled or re-soled when they need it.

Yeah, that's nice. If only I could find them. Is there a pair of black boots within the shores of the United States of America that is different than the others?

Maybe there's a conspiracy among shoe manufacturers, kind of like price-fixing, in that they've all agreed not to make anything different so they don't outdo each other.

Like with cars. Do you know why people like the PT Cruiser and the new Volkswagen Beetle? Oh, they are cute and everything, but the reports say they don't handle well and are uncomfortable.

The PT Cruiser and Beetle look different than every other car within the shores of the United States.

When-I-was-a-kid (in the 1960s and '70s), me and my siblings would sit on my grandmother's porch and watch cars go by (Do not underestimate this as a pastime). We made a game of identifying the cars: Dodges, Chevys, Fords, Lincolns, Oldsmobiles, Jeeps, Darts, Thunderbirds, Falcons, Road Runners, Novas, Corvairs.

Back in the old days, boys and girls, cars had something we used to call "style." This was done by something we used to call "design" of the car's features, like the hood, the headlights and the grill.

We could not play that game today. Cars today are indistinguishable from one another.

You would think in a culture like ours, with its overabundance of everything, that manufacturers of cars and shoes would offer us real choices, not these eeny-meeny-miny-mo choices.

So what happens is that when a real choice does come along, like the PT Cruiser and Beetle, you get all these people wanting something different but they all have the same different thing. Then you have this sub-culture of people who have the same thing. So it ceases to be different.

At this point, I wouldn't mind being part of a sub-culture of women-who-wear-calf-high-black-lace-up-boots. We can meet monthly at a restaurant to plan hot dog sales to raise money for shoeless children in Afghanistan. We can adopt a highway together. We can award pins bearing the length of time we've owned our boots. We can rent buses to travel to stores that sell our kind of boots. We can send out a newsletter with articles on boot care, preserving your laces and the safest way to walk in three-inch heels.

Our mutual enjoyment of lace-up boots will enable us to find true friendship, empower us in our conformity to non-conformity and elevate us above the common folk who wear featureless black boots.

Help!

Automobile Travails of the 1990's

So. I've spent the last five months looking for a new car. Not continuously, day in day out, but looking. Asking. Reading. Thinking.

Since my son totaled my 1992 Tracer (for which I had no collision insurance), I've been driving a 1986 Lancer. Never heard of it? It's the Dodge version of a Chrysler Le Baron, minus the quality control. I bought it because I liked the colors—champagne with a maroon interior.

But it had an oil leak. Minor, at first. A few weeks later I was putting in a quart every four or five days, then two quarts every four or five days, then two quarts every two to three days, then...

I also bought it because I hate interest payments on new cars. I kept driving it with the oil leak. That cost about $5 a week.

Then, pulling into a parking lot one day, a transaxle fell out. That cost $125 to replace. Then we had to replace the other one because, you know, they work together.

One rainy night, the engine started smoking like heck. It was the air conditioner compressor. So now it has no air conditioning.

Then, a week before Christmas, the radiator popped a seam. That cost $350 to replace. Merry Christmas. I took it to Atlanta after New Year's and had to replace the catalytic converter on the way back. That cost $150. Found out the leaking oil was running through the exhaust system.

So I paid someone to replace the valve cover gasket. It still leaked. We tried it again, with stronger gunk to hold it. It still leaked. Again, and it still leaked. Leaks. That cost about $100.

The starter started starting only at certain times, and I started looking more seriously for a new car. I studied religiously the *Consumer's Guide* for new and used cars. I asked people about their cars. I test drove cars.

When I told a car saleswoman I was test driving a number of cars to compare how they performed, she said that was unusual. Many customers, she said, buy a car after just sitting in it, not driving it any-where, because they know what they want before they get there.

I drove five different 1996 cars. One, which I liked the looks of the best, was noisy and leaned on turns. Two others strained noticeably going up hills. Another drove great but was too small.

Only one car had it all. It handled turns and hills with ease, was roomy and fun to drive, and, most important, was a beautiful color—midnight red with a tan interior. It's highly recommended in the guide.

Then I went to the Ford dealer in Staunton, to check how much they'd charge for the same car and give me for my trade-in. They couldn't beat the deal in Harrisonburg. So back I went.

Of course, when you cut a deal for a new car, the salesman asks how much you want to pay per month. Forget the price and the fact that, over five years at 7.9 percent interest, you pay $19,000 for a $14,000 car. I always thought that was sleazy of the salesmen. But two of them told me that's what most of their customers look at, the monthly pay-ments.

The Ford salesman was taken aback that I didn't want the $600 rebate with 7.9 percent interest over five years. I wanted the 2.9 per-cent financing over four years. I'm spending about $25 more per month (which does hurt), but saving over $4000 in interest. And it's a funny thing about that fifth year. It does come.

The day after coming home with my gorgeous new car, my daugh-ter's car broke down in Harrisonburg. It's in for repairs. The Lancer stopped starting at all the following day. My son's Jeep doesn't like starting and, when it does, keeps stalling out. My husband's truck is temporarily off the road. So we have four working adults with one car.

When you get right down to it, take away the premium sound sys-tem, the leather seats, the moonroof, the remote entry system, and the sequential fuel thing-a-ma-jigger, it's just transportation.

Are Guns the Real Problem?

Once there was a little boy who watched cartoons on Saturday morning. The cartoon this four-year-old loved best was *Scooby Doo.*

One day on the program, one of the characters, a ghost, hung himself by the neck on a doorknob. The boy decided he would try it, too. So he tied a cord around the doorknob of his bedroom closet, then put his neck in the loop.

The little boy hung himself and died.

This is a true story. I read the account in a women's magazine—Redbook or McCall's—about 15 years ago.

The boy's mom, fearing her son's three-year-old brother might try the same thing, removed the doorknob. The younger brother, the article said, was still watching *Scooby Doo* on Saturday mornings.

The boy that died had seen doorknobs used all his life—to open and close doors, perhaps to hang a sweater on, or a rubber band. I doubt, until he saw it on his favorite TV show, that it ever occurred to him to use a doorknob to kill himself.

Growing up in the New York City suburb of Long Island, my exposure to guns was rare. Some people collected them, a few used them for hunting ducks out east, but most used them to kill other people—usually in Mafia- or drug-related crimes.

My concept of what guns were used for was developed mostly by reading the headlines of The Daily News and watching TV shows like *Combat, The Rifleman* and *Mannix.*

Guns, I thought, were for killing people.

When I moved to Virginia, I met many people who actually had guns and used them. Guns hung on wall racks or stood in cabinets in their family rooms, were carried in racks in their pick-up trucks.

That was scary. When my husband brought a rifle home, that was even scarier.

He learned to use the gun by setting up a shooting range on our property, shooting toward a cliff and away from the road. In the fall, he went hunting, enjoying the solitude of the woods and occasionally bringing home fresh meat for the dinner table.

I learned to shoot, too, to experience what it was like. I also became capable of defending myself and my little ones should anyone try to hurt me or them while my husband worked at night.

What are guns for?

The average American child ages 2-17 watches 20 hours of television per week, or almost three hours per day. The number of murders they view during those years is 16,000 (*Physician Guide to Media Violence*, AMA, 1996).

Eighty percent of Hollywood executives and 73 percent of Americans believe there is a link between TV violence and real-life violence (MTV national survey, Chicago Tribune, Aug. 13, 1993).

"Train up a child in the way he should go, and when he is old he will not turn from it," says Proverbs 22:6. What are we training our children to do?

The percentage of parents who would like to (but do not) limit their children's TV watching is 73 percent, according to a study reported by Benjamin Barber in a 1993 Harper's magazine story.

Television and movie violence is not the only cause of gun violence, but it is part of it. Other factors, according to a campaign developed by the American Psychological Association and MTV, include:

—The breakdown of the nuclear family. With the divorce rate at 50 percent, many children have no good role models for conflict resolution. Children learn by example, not lectures.

—The absence of a moral compass. In the past, church and synagogue were important influences on children, as were groups like the Boy and Girl Scouts, with moral values at their core.

—Women entering the work force. With both parents working in most families, children have lots of unsupervised time and less parental involvement in their activities.

While gun availability is a factor, it is not the only factor.

Even so, with all the factors put together, gun violence has dropped significantly over the past five years.

According to the Bureau of Justice Statistics, homicides committed with guns by teens have dropped from all-time highs in 1993 and 1994. Children under the age of 14 shot and killed 131 people in 1994. By 1998, that figure had dropped to 54.

Children ages 14-17 shot and killed 3,371 people in 1993, 1,433 in 1998.

Though gun murders have fallen almost 60 percent, the publicity of such incidents has increased. A 1998 survey by TV-Free America showed a 721 percent increase in network news coverage of homicide between 1993 and 1996.

So. What's going on here? It would appear that guns are killing more people than ever before, but it's not so.

It's just not so.

Unfortunately, most people reading this will look at the above-stated facts and still believe the problem is getting worse. The propaganda has done its work.

If gun violence had reached the crisis "they" claim it to be, and the availability of guns was clearly the reason, I would certainly use whatever influence I could to make my children's world a safer place.

In the meantime, I'll continue to show my children and my neighbors what guns—and doorknobs—are for.

English Has, Like, You Know, Evolved Again

Like, fourscore and seven years ago, our forefathers, you know, set forth on this continent a new nation, you know, conceived in liberty and dedicated to the proposition that all men are created, like, equal.

Or like, maybe, ask not what your country can, you know, do for you, but ask rather what you can, you know, do for your country.

If Abraham Lincoln and John Kennedy were college students today, this might be the way they would have framed their immortal statements. But I doubt the statements would have made it to immortality.

I have been trying to figure out how the word "like" has come to figure so prominently in much of America's speech. Although I first noticed it among high school and college students, lately I've heard it from the mouths of many adults. That and, you know, uptalk.

Like seems to have taken the place of the word "said." As in, "The teacher asked me where my homework was and I was like, 'I don't have it.' And he was like, 'Did you do it?' And I was like, 'Yes, but I lost it,' and he was like, 'Well, you'll have to find it.'"

I think it has also taken the place of "um" and "uh," as in the above-quoted presidential statements. It's a filler or something. Some people invoke like so often it suffocates any meaning. Here's a typical conversation between my 17-year-old son and me:

"Mom, can you take me to, like, work?"

"Where do you really want to go?" I reply.

"What do you mean? Like, I just told you, I, like, need to go to work."

"Well, if you mean like as in similar, then where do you want to go that's similar to work?"

"Mom!"

I do this to him and my daughter so often they've become careful about what they say, at least to me. It's become something of a game to catch them at it.

When like is combined with "you know," speech is finally impotent: "I'm like, you know, against that man's politics because, you know, like he's so racist, you know?"

Pretty convincing statement there.

Then there is the phrase I rarely go through a day without hearing: "I was like—wow." The person saying this sounds as if how they felt at that climactic moment is of the utmost importance and then, instead of describing how they felt, they say something as trite as, "I was like—wow." What does that mean? Similar to "wow"? My vocabulary is vanishing?

I realize there are awesome and terrible moments in life when there are no words to say but "wow," but are we all "like—wow" at everything all day?

If the abuse of "like" irritates me like (similar to) a dripping faucet, then uptalk is like chalk screeching on the blackboard. Uptalkers sound to me as if they don't know what they're talking about.

"Hello, my name is Sarah Chumley? I'm a student at John Doe University?" The voice says or asks.

"Yes," I say. (Yes, honey, that's your name. Yes, I've heard of that school—it's two blocks away.)

"I'm in the Sigma Fo sorority? And we're giving a party for mentally challenged citizens at Christmas?" she says or asks.

"Yes," I say again. (I'm reassuring her that there is such a sorority and that I believe her about the party.)

What I feel like saying is, aren't you sure of your name by now or where you go to school? Why are you asking me if you're giving a party? I don't know.

When listening to this type of speech, I keep waiting for a statement, like waiting for a sneeze that never quite happens.

I can't figure out if they talk like this because they a.) are insecure as and need continual affirmation, b.) aren't sure of their material, or c.) think I may feel threatened by something as forceful as a real statement. If the third possibility is true, maybe I should say, "Hey, I'm a secure gal. I can handle a statement. Go ahead. Be bold. Try me."

Callers to the Friday morning *Tag Sale* on WSVA-AM do a variation of this.

"I have a 1987 Dodge for sale? It's an automatic? It's green? It's in good condition? I'm asking $2,000 for it? The number to call is 555-5000." See what I mean? The only information this person seems to be sure of is their phone number. That's good, though, because everybody should at least know their phone number.

When my kids talk this way, (such as, "I was in science class today?") my standard response is, "Are you asking me or telling me?"

Having said all this, I must confess that I do it. Like creeps into my speech—and my writing—here and there. I hope I don't do it often. I don't think I uptalk at all. But then, like, you know, I don't have to listen to myself?

Unrecognized Prejudices Color World An Unreal Hue

In a conversation the other day, a colleague made a derogatory reference to "all the little right-wing activists" running around a certain nearby campus.

His remark told me more about him than about the political activities on campus. It put me in mind of the camera that copies color photos into the black-and-white prints we use in the newspaper. It has a red lens, so it doesn't see red. A reddish complexion comes out white.

You see, my colleague looks at the political activity on campus through his left-wing lenses, making the left-wingers turn white and the right-wingers stand out in contrast.

We all look at life through the lenses of our prejudices, our bigotries. The thing is to remember that our lenses are colored.

I find it difficult to rid myself of my prejudices, but I can at least be aware of them. Exist in here with them. Laugh and cry at them at the appropriate times.

Like the interview I did a few weeks ago.

Tears dripped down the minister's cheeks as he told me about the souls he'd won, the lives that had been changed…in particular, about a young woman who'd suffered from panic attacks who could now sing a song in front of the congregation.

I came away from that interview changed, too.

I tend to prejudge ministers. I won't get into why. Let's just say the title "Rev." doesn't automatically inspire my respect. But after 10 months as the religion reporter here—dealing with ministers of many persuasions on a daily basis—I've learned to at least maintain an open mind about them. When I encounter humility, honesty and sincere devotion, it stays open. But in the presence of pride, insincerity and dogmatism it snaps closed.

But everybody deserves a chance. If they don't matter, I don't matter.

Some people, because they find it necessary to think of themselves as free of prejudice, have taken up the cause of the poor, the homeless, the blacks, the women, the whatever...and have taken "sides" against the affluent, the employed, the white, the men, the whatever. You know, the reverse prejudice thing.

Though the justification for this is wonderful, it's the same sin, the exact same sin. And what makes it any more virtuous when "A" does it than when "B" does it?

Feminism would have been much more attractive to me years ago if it were not characterized by prejudice against men. The oppressed in this case would like to do some oppressing of their own.

Like Susan McClary, a "musicologist who relates the creation of musical works to their social context." Reader's Digest (December 1995) reported that McClary was given a "genius grant" of at least $250,000 by the MacArthur Foundation to devote herself to finding the phallic themes, patriarchal violence and the "necessary purging or containment of the female" in classical music.

McClary's research uncovered "the throttling murderous rage of a rapist incapable of attaining release" in Beethoven's Ninth Symphony, just by listening to it.

"We do not judge great art. It judges us," said Dr. Caroline Gordon. And McClary's conclusions tell me more about her than they do about Beethoven (who, conveniently, is not here to defend himself). Just as my colleague's comment on right-wingers told me more about him than campus politics.

Not that I haven't had my share of patriarchal oppression. My father—God bless him—dominated our household through fear. But interpreting life in defiance of that oppression keeps me in subjection to it as surely as succumbing to it.

Prejudices? I've got plenty of them. I've never had rose-colored glasses, but I do have a pair of yellow-tinted sunglasses. All the pasture, mountains and trees look vibrantly green through them.

The thing to remember is that my glasses are colored.

Me? Intolerant?

I heard the preacher's voice come on the call-in radio show.

"Well, now…" he started. I knew what was coming next. A know-it-all rebuttal—complete with scripture and reference—to a previous caller's remarks.

This preacher and others like him have no tolerance for any other point of view and they waste no time whacking off their perceived enemy's head with a scripture or a statistic or some final word on the subject.

I extend a finger and mash the radio button off. Humph. I have no tolerance for such people.

In a similar vein, the United States Senate officially condemned Bob Jones University in a statement introduced by Sen. Robert Torricelli (D-N.J.). The statement, supported by the Interfaith Alliance, denounced the totally privately-funded university for discriminating against and dividing Americans "on the basis of race, ethnicity and religion."

In a similar vein, the New York Knicks decided after nine years to stop training in Charleston, S.C. The NBA team said it will not hold its playoff training camp there because of the Confederate flag controversy. The NAACP is leading a tourism boycott of South Carolina until the flag is removed from the Statehouse dome.

In a similar vein, in Michigan, American Family Association leader Gary Glenn filed a complaint with police about comments made by Ferndale councilman Craig Covey, a homosexual activist, after last month's defeat of an ordinance that would have granted gays special rights. Covey told supporters that the vote "shows that the Christian Right is down but not yet out. We might have to drive another dagger into that vampire."

In a similar vein, a recent letter-to-the-editor in the Daily News-Record came from a woman who was angry at hearing the name of Christ used in prayer at a public meeting.

Which only goes to show, that the perception of intolerance breeds intolerance.

Welcome to the new improved intolerance. In this up-to-date version, it is cool to voice your hurt or angry feelings when offended by white American Christians. It is chic to critique them.

What's new and improved about the new intolerance, is that it's passing for tolerance. The new intolerance is gushingly fascinated darling with all of our wonderfully diverse cultures and religions except white American Christianity.

It's the old log-in-eye syndrome. You know, where you take the splinters from others eyes while you've got a log in your own.

Log-in-eye is blinding. All you can see is the log. Especially susceptible to log-in-eye are those of us who defy the status quo. It's an easy trap to fall into.

To give a simple example, when I first moved to Virginia, my family of four attended a small church around the corner from our apartment. On one of our first visits, we slid into an unoccupied pew near the front.

A few minutes later, another family stood in the aisle staring at us. "We always sit here," they said. We slid down and they squished in, though most of the other pews were empty.

I think this habit of sitting in the same pew or row is silly, so when I go to church, I always sit someplace different. Because I am not religious. Ha.

I did this for years before I realized that my anti-religion was a religion itself.

The best way to overcome log-in-eye is to carry a big mirror. And if that log blinds you from seeing yourself, ask someone who will be honest with you. Usually that's the person you instinctively don't want to ask.

You should ask yourself the questions you'd rather dismiss:

Am I fighting intolerance with intolerance? Fighting bigotry with bigotry? Fighting hate with hate? Am I part of the problem? Am I perpetuating the problem?

Another question would be, "What is my goal?" Is it to sow the seeds that will bring about lasting change? Or is it to broadcast to the world that "I'm not going to take this lying down?"

Now, I don't expect the U.S. Senate or the New York Knicks to be agents of justice and peace, but I do expect it of individuals who profess to be moving toward those goals.

The mystic writer Evelyn Underhill wrote, "The saintly and simple Cure d'Ars was once asked the secret of his abnormal success in converting souls. He replied that it was done by being very indulgent to others and very hard on himself; a recipe which retains all its virtue still."

The Dilemma of Being White

I've been white all my life.

Unlike my friend Sarah, who, when we sang Beatles' songs together on the school bus in third grade, was "colored." Those who knew better called her Negro. In high school, she was Afro-American.

By the time Sarah reached her mid-20s, she was black, then in her late 30s, African American. In some circles, she is a "woman of color."

Being white is so generic.

Look at the form for Census 2000, item 9. Look at the choices of race:

White; Black, African American, or Negro; American Indian or Alaska Native; Asian Indian; Chinese; Filipino; Japanese; Korean; Vietnamese; Native Hawaiian; Guamanian or Chamorro; Samoan; other Pacific Islander.

Question 8, asks if the person is Spanish/Hispanic/or Latino. If so, the choices are: Mexican, Mexican American, or Chicano; Puerto Rican; Cuban; or other.

Everyone has specific choices—some, not only of "race," but vocabulary preference—except whites.

It doesn't seem fair—everyone else is referred to by their people group, their ancestral lineage, their culture of origin, but me? I'm tagged by my skin color. Lumped with all the other white-skinned people on the planet.

Actually, the census question has nothing to do with race. If it were, the choices would be Caucasoid, Negroid or Mongoloid, according to the definition in Webster's New World Dictionary.

Race is inappropriate when applied to cultural, religious or national groups, says the Columbia Concise Encyclopedia. The only reference to race on the census form is Negro.

Though the first option—white—should set the precedent for skin color, it does not. If it did, the other choices would be black, yellow, red…brown? The only group identified strictly by skin color is white.

Unlike whites, black-skinned people have the option of identifying with their ancestors' cultural group (African) as well as their current national group (American), or with their race (Negro).

The remaining choices are national and cultural groups. At first I thought the census was trying to get a handle on where immigrant groups have settled. If that's the case, don't the white immigrants matter? What about all the Eastern Europeans that have settled in the U.S. in the past 10 years? What about those from the Middle East?

Perhaps I am showing my ignorance. Obviously, dividing white-skinned people into sub-groups serves no purpose.

I sometimes wonder how identifying myself more specifically would change my concept of myself and my relationship with other whites.

My multiple-great grandfather, Paul Sandstrom, worked his way from Sweden to New York City on a merchant ship in the early 1800s. Thus I could identify myself as a Nordic American.

But I wonder: Would I feel a kinship with other Nordic Americans? Less connection with white-skinned people of differing origins? Should I learn more about the culture and customs of the Nordic people in order to attain a stronger sense of heritage and identity?

It's been so many generations since my grandfather migrated here. The only reminder I have of my Swedish heritage is my big rectangular head.

(Like, I'll be walking through a fine department store when I notice a rack of gorgeous women's hats. I always fall in love with one. But when I try it on, it perches atop my head rather than sliding down to where it belongs.

"Oh man, I wish my head wasn't so big," I sigh, wishing I inherited my skull genes from my mother.)

Mom's side of the family tree would be even more difficult to identify with. The Thompsons immigrated to the New World from England in the 1600s.

According to my old Encyclopedia International, the ethnic group originating in the British Isles is properly known as Atlanto-Mediterranean. Hmmm...

To be fair to both parental lineages, I should be inclusive.

If my answer to question 9 on Census 2000 was consistent with the other choices of "race," I'd check the box that says "Some other race." And write in the blank: Nordic Atlanto-Mediterranean American.

Who do I think I'm kidding? I'm just a white girl.

How Much Is Enough?

Looking back, I suppose my first real home after getting married was shoddy.

Almost all our furniture was given to us. An orange vinyl easy chair, a brown recliner, a tufted golden loveseat. Of course, everyone made sure we had a TV set, so we had three used ones.

Before moving into this old house, we lived for three months in an efficiency unit on Sayville (N.Y.) dock. We often fetched our dinner off the dock with a crab net. The seafood market owners sometimes gave us leftover shrimp.

We had no car, no telephone. We made vacations out of bus trips to distant towns, where we would just walk around and window shop. On Sundays, we loved going to flea markets with friends.

At Christmas, the husband crafted gifts with his woodworking tools, while I stitched others at my sewing machine.

I'm sure this is quite foolish to today's newlyweds. Everything is so planned. They have it so together: each finishes their college education and purchase new cars; they build houses and fill them with carpet and furniture, appliances and stereos and new television sets.

The objective is what I question. Are they building a foundation for a relationship that will last a lifetime, or a domestic facility in which to warehouse all their consumer goods? Are they wedded lovers or co-consumers?

"The wife in curlpapers is replaced by the wife who puts on lipstick before she wakens her husband...but having two bathrooms ruined the capacity to cooperate."—Margaret Mead, anthropologist.

A friend of mine spent a few weeks this spring driving around Germany and Italy. He said the homes in the villages were well built but unpretentious. Most of the cars were small and not new.

The townspeople owned or worked in the villages' small shops or on outlying farms. No one's in a hurry. All have time to chat for a few minutes.

My friend said, "It's like they are living for something else."

He could have been talking about another planet. Live for something else? What else is there to live for?

No matter how detached I think I am from American culture, it affects me. I have never known anything else. Who am I kidding?

So what if I watch TV for only an hour a week? Or see a whole movie only once every month or two? So what if I shun shopping at the SuperGlom in favor of a locally owned store? I live in the USA, was born and raised here, indoctrinated since birth with the philosophies of consumerism and materialism.

Consumerism is a socio-economic theory that a continual increase in the consumption of goods is sound.

Materialism—the spiritual doctrine that comfort, pleasure and wealth are the only or highest goals or values—forms the base upon which we make our most important decisions. It guides us toward when to marry, how many children to have and determines our life's work.

Do we choose a career because it's something we are gifted at, because it will enrich or serve mankind? Or because it pays well?

How about children? Do we decide to not have children so we can have more stuff for ourselves? Do we base our decision on how many children to have on the amount of love we have to give or how many college educations we can afford to finance?

And then what are we training our children for? What is the objective of their obtaining a college degree? To become good neighbors or good consumers?

"Men who are not free always idealize their bondage," wrote Boris Pasternak.

We think ourselves so wise.

Nietzche said, "If you want to have it easy in life, stay with the herd."

What if we were to live for something else, such as my friend experienced in German and Italian villages? What would we live for? What can we live for? Can we define our own reality in the midst of the cult of prosperity?

Once you have found the answer to these questions, you will never feel at home here again.

Body Language

o o o o o o o o o o o o o o o o o o o o o o o o o o o o o o o o
"And when I run, I feel His pleasure."

> —*Eric Liddle in "Chariots of Fire"*

Thoughts While Walking. 11 July 1998.

What a beautiful morning. So clear and clean and blue.

Gosh, I have so much to do today. Should I take the two mile road. Let's see, that takes almost an hour. No, I'll go by Kay's and do a 40-minute walk. Besides it's prettier with the woods and the river.

I wonder if those giant bugs will bother me again. Sometimes they're there and sometimes they're not. I hope it's not too shady this way. It's actually chilly this morning.

I need to keep my pace up so I can feel my heart pump. Lengthen your back, head straight up, stomach pulled in. There, good. Now if I can only walk this fast while daydreaming.

I wonder what he's doing with that pile of dirt on the bank. Gee, he has lots of plants in his yard but nothing around his front porch, no shrubs or anything. Maybe he's going to build something there.

We should have a special "Dan's back" dinner since he's moved back in. Just the family. But the family isn't all home at the same time. It would be a big deal just to get everyone home for this meal. I should bake a cake at least. But I don't want to heat up the house with the oven. And who's going to end up eating the cake? Me. Forget it.

I wonder why Kay has the fence posts on the outside of the fence. Maybe it's better for the horses to have it smooth on the inside. Or so she has a nice view from inside the pasture. Gee that's a long fence. It must have cost her a fortune. Although she did have those Craig boys do the work.

Her house has such a view of all the mountains. I wonder why the people who built our house didn't think about the view. But maybe there was a view of the mountains a hundred years ago, and the woods grew up later. That's the first thing I would do when I build a house, make sure it has a grand view; with lots of big windows.

Ann said some relative of hers has a new house she built with just a few windows and views of the mountains all around her but heavy drapes on the windows. How can anyone just close themselves in like that. She thinks it's frivolous to look at the view.

Gosh what sense does life make without beauty?

Oh Jesus (coming around the bend overlooking the Blue Ridge Mountains), it's so beautiful.

The clouds have settled into the hollows and the mountains are blue-gray, like slate, as far as I can see to the south and north. I don't think there's anywhere in the world more beautiful than this right now.

Wish I could take a picture of this so I can have it with me always. Gosh they got a lot of hay from this pasture. Look at all those bales. Like shredded wheat biscuits.

I wonder why they don't have sheep in the field this year. It looks so cool by the river here. The maple guardians of the river, like sentries, are so lush with leaves. They swell like ocean waves when the wind comes through, the creation giving praise to God.

I want to be part of it. I wish I could lift my arms and fly over the river and be blown by the air currents and the wind.

If I had my journal I'd climb that dirt path and settle down with my back against that tree. I'd sit on that hill and write, just write all day. Get up a stretch and walk around and sit and write.

But I have no time for such things anymore. So much to do. What does any of it matter?

I wonder if that's what Wordsworth did, if he sat outside and wrote. Or did he remember everything and go home to write?I wish I could remember all the lofty things I think while I'm walking. Like that poem I wrote during the flood when the river was wild and free and hilarious, touching the treetops and breaking the rules about where it belonged.

Maybe I should carry a small tape recorder and say what I'm thinking so I can transcribe it when I get home. Hmm.

It's hard to believe the world is in a state of decay with all this vibrant green life. What was it like before it became polluted with the sins of man? It's glorious now.

I can understand why Walt Whitman could write so much just from glorying in a blade of grass.

Here's this hill again. Work those muscles. It feels good to work them, to feel my heart pounding in my chest, to get out of breath.

The woods are damp and quiet. I'd like to sit on the silent needles or better yet lie on them and try to see the sky through the thick pines. To just sit in all the dark silence. Someone must have planted the trees here, they're so perfectly in line.

Mmm. A nice place to die or just to lie down and fall asleep.

> *The woods are lovely, dark, and deep,*
> *But I have promises to keep,*
> *And miles to go before I sleep,*
> *And miles to go before I sleep.*

> —Robert Frost

Root Canals And The Language Only Dentists Understand

Root canal No. 3.

Though people felt sorry for me because I was getting a root canal, I felt as long as that dentist is using Novocain, it couldn't be too bad. My first root canal was done without it.

The aged dentist believed root canals were best performed without dulling the nerves.

"Tell me when it hurts," he said. "That's how I'll know when to stop."

It didn't take much to indicate my pain. The dentists I've had since then have said that guy was nuts.

Actually, I'm not tracking too badly. My mother was wearing dentures at my age. I brush and floss and everything, but I end up with these problems anyway. The philosophy of dentistry must have changed in the intervening years. Whenever I ask if a tooth is worth saving, the response is always "Yes, we must try."

Regular dentists perform some root canals, but when the job is complex, as in the case of rear molars, they'll refer you to an endodontist. This is a person who makes his living doing root canals.

A root canal is a big deal in the life of a tooth. I think it kills it.

There's nothing to be nervous about getting a root canal. What hurts most is the two-foot hypodermic needle the dentist sticks into your gum as he shoots it full of Novocain, sometimes in a couple of different places.

After a few minutes you're numb. He then stakes a sheet of plastic (kind of a dental condom) over your wide-open mouth, making a hole to expose the infected tooth. Then he asks you questions about your job. Not "yes" and "no" questions, but about what you do.

"So what do you write at the newspaper?" he asked.

"Ah-ums, ea-ures an uh e-i-jun age," I said. He, being a dentist, understood this.

"No offense, but I never read the religion page," he said.

Then he pulled out the drill.

To begin, the endodontist drills an opening into the pulp chamber of the decayed tooth.

As he did this, he told me about a dentist who was convinced that patients felt pain from this only because of the noise of the drill. So, rather than Novocain, he gave them Walkmans and their favorite music to listen to as he drilled.

The endodontist said he once had a patient who wrote a column for the religion page, and tried to think of her name. I named a few of my predecessors, but he shook his head.

"Onnie Ar-neh Iffett?" I said, thinking he was mixing her up with the Valley Banner columnist.

"No," he said.

Next the dentist reams out the tissue from the root canal, all the way down to the gum, with small instruments that look like sewing needles with the tip broken off. This takes an awful long time. I mean, he's just banging this thing in and out of your tooth for like an hour. He told me to shut my mouth whenever he takes his hand out.

I wish he'd told me that last time. My jaw was dislocated for about five weeks after he did a root canal six years ago. It popped back while I was at the movies, watching *Dances With Wolves*. You know, the part when Kevin Costner is talking to the commander of the outpost who later shoots himself.

Reaming, reaming. The dentist had an oldies radio station on and decided to play "Name That Tune." The guy knows every song that's been recorded since 1960 and he's pretty cocky about it, too. So he was the only one having fun.

Reaming, reaming.

When he took his hand out I asked, "Ahvent ooh otten any basteh at diz in zix yeehs?"

He laughed. Actually, for such a dreaded procedure, his games and conversation do take the edge off.

When the tooth is empty of life, the dentist installs silver wires to keep it in your gum, then fills it with cement. Finally, he uses a soldering gun to seal it with a sizzling hot and stinky substance.

After many days, my tooth no longer hurts. But it feels like because of being wholer now it's squishing my other teeth together and my front teeth tickle.

The only quote about dentists in *The Oxford Dictionary of Quotations* is this by Oscar Wilde: "It is very vulgar to talk like a dentist when one isn't a dentist. It produces a false impression."

So, if I have given the false impression that I really know what the dentist is doing during a root canal, please forgive my vulgarity.

Eating By the Book. Which Book?

A blop of margarine melts in the cast iron frying pan. When it has liquefied, three jumbo eggs are cracked into it.

On the burner behind it, four slices of bacon are crisping to a perfect brown crackle. The other front burner heats yet another iron pan, cooking a large pan of potatoes in a generous pool of canola oil and more margarine for home fries.

When the toast is done, a third of a stick of butter is swathed onto two slices.

Boy's food.

This is a typical meal for the husband in my house. Typical ever since I've known him, which has been almost 30 years.

Yet his cholesterol readings—taken again weeks ago—are terrific. The bad cholesterol is low, below the normal range. The good cholesterol is normal.

The guy is a testimonial to the benefits of eating bacon, greasy cheeseburgers and hot dogs.

At 46, you'd think a lifetime of eating like that would show up in a cholesterol test. It just confirms my belief that all human beings are not created identical.

Not everyone should eat low fat diets. As a matter of fact, few people should. Ever notice how fat-reduced foods cost more than those that have not been tampered with?

Get the connection here: many foods are offered in fat-free or low-fat forms, they dominate the supermarket, they cost more and we are told on commercials, news shows, radio talks shows, billboards, in magazines, books and pamphlets to consume them.

One plus one equals two. Hmm. Could it be a marketing ploy?

The latest thing in diets is the carbohydrate wars. Throughout the 80's and 90's, "they" sold us on a diet high in complex carbohydrates: plenty of pasta, rice and bread. The recommended proportions of protein, fats and carbs given by the USDA, doctors and diet book authors were all the same for every human being on the planet.

Then a few years ago a new diet fad was re-introduced, containing few carbs, high in protein. The high-carb people went into attack mode. Books, articles, speeches, conventions and more studies all came out refuting—even claiming as dangerous—the "new" low-carb diet.

In actuality, some people (gasp!) operate better with less carbs and a bit more protein. Some people's bodies function better with more carbs.

Could it be that we are all not exactly the same?

Public education has done its best to make obedient uniform citizens of us.

All people at the age of four can recognize shapes, count to 30, skip, share toys, know in from out, top from bottom and up from down. Through all the grades of school, each individual child is expected to know exactly the same information, be capable of the same physical skills, and display the same social characteristics as all the other children at his age level.

Woe to the child who does not keep up with the conformity. He is "learning disabled" or "ADD" or "hyperactive." He must be given drugs in order to put a lid on his natural tendencies to run, jump, explore, question, play, work.

Sitting at a school desk all day, producing the same worksheets as our classmates, trains us to perform boring computer work, to machine the same parts all day, to sit in the same chair, to stand in the same spot.

Doing as we're told by pseudo-authorities—"experts"—and following the example of selected role models—celebrities—trains us to be good consumers and citizens.

Yes, we will all buy 2 or 1½ percent milk.

Yes, we will all buy a minivan or SUV.

Yes, we will all go to Disney World or Myrtle Beach.

Yes, we will all buy cell phones.

Yes, we will all purchase movies on videotape.

Yes, we will all collect Pokemon cards.

And all the restaurants in every town in America will be the same. Each main street will have a McDonald's and Burger King, an Applebee's and a Shoney's, an Outback and a Texas Steakhouse.

And we will all eat at those restaurants.

As for me and my house, we will cross the state line and head to Brandywine, W.Va.

There we will have breakfast—consisting of a couple of eggs, a mess of home fries, biscuit and gravy and a pile of pancakes—for about $4. The people are friendly and the service is great.

It's called Fat Boy's Pork Palace.

Am I trying to incite a rebellion? Yes.

How Long Must I Sing This Song?

Gosh it's taking a long time to heal.

How does one achieve a prolapsed, herniated, slipped, ruptured, squished-out disk? That is a question.

Most people can point to an event and say, this is how I threw out my back: lifting the remote control to the TV set, bending over to blow dry my hair or carrying 17 plastic grocery sacks at once.

I have no such event.

But my lifestyle, now that's something to take a look at. Over the past six years, there have been some big changes in my everyday habits. When I lived out in the holler, I heated and cooked on woodstoves. That meant splitting wood, carrying it into the house and loading it into the stove. I baked bread from scratch: stirring, kneading, rolling.

Hung clothes outside on the line. Stacked hundreds of hay bales in the barn. Ran for miles and miles daily. Pulled huge ticks off the dog. On weekends, hiked or rode horseback or cut firewood.

Since I got this job (I'm not complaining about it, just making some observations) I spend most weekdays sitting. Since I got my motorcycle license, I spend most weekends sitting.

According to the scientific chart shown to me by a bona fide certified physical therapist, sitting puts more strain on your back than scaling the Sears Tower, jumping with a pogo stick or almost any other activity known to man. Hmm.

The lower back pain began soon after I began my sit-down job. Every now and then. Nothing serious. Pop a couple aspirin, lay on the heating pad and it was OK.

However, after I began riding motorcycles, the occasional pain was accompanied by slight numbness in the foot. Better check it out.

Thus began my first venture deep into the world of medicine. Heck, just getting the correct diagnosis took three months. Getting a misdiagnosis and being treated for the wrong ailment was not a good experience. In fact it was very bad.

Instead of swimming out to sea, I became a beached whale. My mild occasional symptoms intensified to constant pain.

So.

I did not venture out to visit another expert for six weeks after this experience. When I did, it was because I was spending most of each night awake and crying.

The physical therapy (moist heat, massage, traction, exercise), entailed three visits a week for two and a half months. And, oh yes, the medicine: the non-steroid anti-inflammatory and sleep aid, followed by oral prednisone and finally cortisone shots.

I'm not saying all this to impress anyone. Others and their pets have gone through much more and I don't want to hear about it. Call, write or stop me on the street to discuss good health.

Water has always been my cure-all for everything. Lots of it. Really. And eating fruits and veggies. Fresh air. Moving and doing. I am an extremely healthy person.

Though it has been humbling to have to depend on people who know more than me about my condition, I still question everything. Everything.

My PT says to me, he says, "Gee, you ask a lot of questions."

Like when my M.D. first suggested I get cortisone injections, I said, "No way. Not an option." The only thing I knew about cortisone was outdated stuff from 1980s running magazines.

When she brought it up again, I agreed to "be open" to it. I spoke with my PT, then another PT. I researched cortisone on the John Hopkins and other websites. I asked people how getting the shot had helped them. I spoke with the anesthesiologist.

Still trying to decide, I asked a friend in church to pray for me. He said, "Well, I'll pray for you, but…." He then told me about his wife getting the shot for her back, the relief she experienced and how she regretted deferring it for so long.

So. By the time I got that shot I was well informed and in a positive state of mind, although my doctors and therapists may have been plotting my demise by then.

Along with all the months of therapy, it helped me feel 75 percent better.

Through all of this, my vision of complete healing has never faltered. Thank God for my PTs, who have all said I can run again. Thank God for my family and friends who have believed with me.

And thank God for Jesus, who spent very little time sitting.

Um, What's An MRI?

Hey, baby, how about an MRI?

That's not exactly how I was told to get an MRI. It was more like, "Uh oh, time for an MRI."

To which I replied, "What is an MRI, anyway?"

Until now, I've gotten away with not knowing what an MRI was. Whenever anyone talked about getting an MRI, I just figured it was some fancy new way of doing x-rays.

I am reluctantly becoming acquainted with the language of medicine. As little as I can get by with.

When someone asks about the anti-inflammatory drug I'm taking, I say, "I don't know. It starts with an N."

And the drug that helps you sleep? "I don't know. It starts with a D."

My paradigm has always been one of health. It still is. Some people seem to thrive on sickness, their own and others. If everyone was healthy, they'd have nothing to do, nothing to talk about. Nobody would need them.

In spite of what I'm undergoing, I don't plan to become an expert in modern medicinal terminology and treatments. But the MRI was sure an interesting experience.

I was asked a bunch of questions about metal, whether I have any inside me, like bullets or metal shavings or steel pins holding me together. I said no, but I wondered if I had implants that I didn't know about, like Scully on "X Files."

They also asked if I was claustrophobic and I said no but then I remembered being locked in my grandmother's bathroom when I was four and how long it had taken my uncle to break down the door and how scared I was.

They asked if I could lay flat on my back for a half-hour. I lied, "Yes."

Once I'd taken off my ring and earrings and slipped into hospital garb, I had a short wait and then was shown to the MRI drawer.

"I'm going inside of that?" I asked.

"Hmm, hmm," nodded the aide and the technician.

I climbed onto the table. The teckie asked what kind of music I wanted to listen to. "Classical will do," I said.

He put headphones on me and slid me into the tunnel. It was warm inside, yellowish. The ceiling was about six inches from my nose. I wondered what they do with real fat people, how they get them in there.

Over the cheesy headphones, the techie tuned in some garbled Enya. Not exactly what I asked for. I couldn't even tell what song she was singing. Soon the volume was turned down and a voice said, "Ma'am? Could you move about two inches to your right?"

I squiggled over.

Then again. "Ma'am? Could you move about an inch toward your head?"

I squiggled up. Then waited for something to happen.

Ever see the movie, *Soylent Green*? I felt like the old guy lying on the table listening to classical music, waiting for the gentle drugs to kill him.

And then like Mr. Spock after he died in the *Star Trek* movie and they jettisoned his body in the casket out of the Enterprise. I imagined I was in this tube, floating around in outer space.

My back and right leg were starting to hurt—the disk and nerve problem I was in there for. I wondered if the pain would get so bad that I'd have to press the little ball to signal I wanted out. Then I remembered the 24th mile of the 1989 Marine Corps Marathon.

The vibrating and banging started. *Rrr-rrr-rrr-rrr. Rrr-rrr-rrr-rrr. Wank wank wank wank wank. Rrr-rrr-rrr-rrr. Wank wank wank wank.*

"Maybe just being in this will make me all better," I thought.

Let's see, I should write a column for Father's Day. What can I write about Dad, I thought. Hmm. He was no spiritual leader in the family. Couldn't hold a job or keep a business going. I need something posi-

tive and uplifting, I thought. Well, he was generous, extravagant sometimes. He was funny....

What if I get stuck in here? I wondered if the mechanism ever broke
that slid out the drawer. But then I felt cool air at my feet and began
sliding back out into the world.

So from what I understand, an MRI uses magnetic and radio waves
to create images of tissue and muscle and other stuff inside you.
Nuclear magnetic resonance.

In other words, a fancy new way to do x-rays.

Looking for Healing

But God chose the foolish things of this world to confound the wise.

That's been the story of my life.

This particular chapter of that story began in February 1999, when I consulted a chiropractor for some mild back pain. The occasional pain did not concern me, but the tingling and numbness in my right foot did. That signaled some nerve involvement.

The chiropractor made an instant diagnosis. As he gave me an adjustment, he said, "It hurts the worst when you get up in the morning, right?"

"No," I said. "It doesn't hurt in the morning at all." It hurt only when I exercised, like fast walking or running, or worked hard, like shoveling or scrubbing the floor.

Well. After the third adjustment, it did hurt in the morning. It hurt all night, so that I could not sleep more than an hour at a time. I could not lie on my back.

I hoped it would go away, but it got worse. By April I felt brave enough to see a doctor, this time a medical doctor. She prescribed two medicines—for pain and relaxation—and recommended physical therapy.

Three times a week I underwent physical therapy, which included traction, ultrasound massage, nerve mobility, hardening exercises and pool therapy. Each visit lasted two hours or more.

When by July I was no better, my doctor ordered an MRI and blood tests, then cortisone pills, then cortisone shots.

All this time I was a reluctant patient, cooperating with the physical therapy, but hating the drugs, the long-range harm they were doing to my body. Of course, all the drugs promoted weight gain. Combined with my forced inactivity, I gained 20 pounds, which logic told me further hurt my back.

I had numerous diagnosis, and was unsure which one was correct: slipped disk? arthritis? myofascial disorder? sacro-iliac joint degeneration? scoliosis? The symptoms for all of these were there.

I researched various treatments for these diagnosis, because when it comes to my health, I am a take-charge person. But I didn't know what the problem was, so I could not decide on a plan of action. You don't treat arthritis the way you treat a slipped disk.

The cortisone shots (three over two months) helped ease some pain and in September I was released from physical therapy. But I still hurt. I still could not lie on my back.

By November it had worsened. I could sleep only in a tight fetal position on my left side. In December, I began seeing a highly recommended chiropractor.

He helped. By mid-January I was sleeping better.

A few weeks later it suddenly got worse. Worse and different than it had been before. I could not stand up straight. My back was twisted, subjected to constant spasms. I could not walk, only shuffle. Driving my car was so painful.

One morning I had an interview at a downtown coffee shop. I hobbled from the Daily News-Record across the street to the parking lot and stopped. It hurt too much to walk. I stood and cried.

My chiropractor was at a loss. He sent me to a pain specialist. The pain specialist ordered another MRI. But first I had to see my family doctor for a referral.

My doctor, concerned about a correct diagnosis, stopped the MRI, prescribed strong pain relievers and muscle relaxers told me he would contact me with the results of my tests.

They came back negative: no arthritis.

By this time, I was so discouraged, I decided to do nothing.

Looking for Healing (Part II)

Then, two months later, my husband and I went to a fund-raising dinner. He was my human crutch as we entered the banquet room. That's when I ran into Dee, an acquaintance who practiced massage therapy. Two people had told me of being healed under her care.

I threw myself into her arms.

"Oh, Dee," I cried. "I need you."

For a year I'd been getting treatment for back pain. I'd seen two chiropractors, two medical doctors and a physical therapist, taken oral and been injected with various steroid and non-steroid drugs, gotten an MRI, x-rays and blood tests

I had prayed and been prayed for. My faith in God's good will assured me that life would again be free of pain. How and when that would happen, I did not know.

After a column I wrote last year about this problem, a reader sent me a collection of articles and notes from various Christian traditions about healing in the Bible. I was reminded of God's promises to heal, read about instances in the Bible and contemporary life in which he healed the sick. In the New Testament, nowhere did Jesus deny healing to anyone who came to him.

I did have my doubts. At one point, I tried to pump some "reality" into my thinking. Looking myself square in the eye (in the bathroom mirror), I admonished me to forget about ever running again. Walking would have to suffice.

Not that there's anything wrong with walking. But I am, and will be while I breathe, a runner.

But by February 2000, walking was no longer an option. Twisted and limping, I could not walk a few feet without great pain. Sitting hurt. Standing hurt. Sleeping hurt.

Dee practiced neuromuscular massage and had chosen not to be certified, so my insurance would not pay for treatments. Big deal.

She had a friendly cottage on her property where she saw her clients. As we stood talking, she looked me over.

Suddenly she said, "It's your piriformis muscle."

She pointed to a colorful poster on the wall, to a small muscle deep in the buttock that connects the hip to the sacrum. She showed me where the sciatica nerve ran alongside the piriformis. My tight, spasming piriformis was pinching the major nerve running down my leg into my foot, causing pain, numbness and tingling.

She showed me other muscles being affected by my "angry" piriformis, one running up the center of my back.

"Muscle moves bone," she said.

The spasming muscles had pulled my spine into a C shape. As a matter of fact, a few practitioners had diagnosed me with curvature of the spine. But I knew that was not right.

Dee said I won the award for being her worst case ever. She also said I would heal completely.

Before starting, Dee prayed for guidance, not in a pretentious sort of way, but in humble acknowledgement that God knew exactly what was afflicting me and that he, ultimately, would do the healing.

Improvement was slow but measurable. We celebrated the victories as they came: standing up straight, walking without difficulty, sleeping all night. One day in early May I realized there was no more sciatica pain.

By July 11, the last time I saw Dee, I'd started running.

Running. It was more like shuffling, interspersed with walking. I measure the victories: one mile, one mile without walking; two miles, two miles without walking; this week I've been running three miles without walking.

I am grateful, so grateful, to be able to sleep all night, to shop for groceries, to drive my car without hurting. But the grand prize is running. In the midst of the worst pain, this is the picture I saw, that I could not talk myself out of: me running.

Deeper than the reality of the affliction was the reality of God's goodness, of his promise to heal and, expressed in the hands and words of my friend Dee, his great love.

Running for My Life

I ran today.

I am no Olympic runner. I do not run fast, but I have great endurance. I have never won a race, but I have always finished.

I began running on June 10, 1979. My friend Ravonne asked me to join her daily 6:30 a.m. runs. I met her faithfully each morning, pulled out of bed by my obligation to her. After a month, I could run (without walking) the hilly three-eighths mile route.

One morning at the end of July, I said goodbye, as usual, to Ravonne when we reached her house and headed home. But when I reached my corner, rather than turning left, I went straight. Straight up the hill for three blocks. Then I turned right, and ended up running the perimeter of Shenandoah's east end.

That's the day I became a runner. For the first time, I had stayed disciplined at something long enough for it to change me.

The discipline began to seep into other parts of my life—housework, study habits, relationships. I'd always been impulsive, starting projects but never finishing them. That changed too, which, in turn, altered my perception of who I was, what I was capable of.

To train for a marathon in 1989, I had to find new routes for long runs. The Weaver hollow road would add five miles. Plus, it was a dirt road (easy on the joints) and followed the creek (tranquil). It started with a ½-mile, 45-degree climb, which looked monstrous. I needed that hill to strengthen my "quads" for the final miles of the 26.2-mile race.

I decided to assault it in increments. Twice a week, I ran a quarter of the way further than the previous time. At the end of the second week, I topped it, lifted my arms and shouted "Yay!"

An artist I once interviewed said his practice of karate directly influenced his creativity, though he could not explain how. Neither can I explain how the physical activity affects our mental, as well as our spiritual or creative capacities; or what element in the exercise is the catalyst that effects the transfusion with our other parts. But it happens.

"With flesh, that hath so little time to stay, And yields mere base-ment for the soul's emprise, Expect prompt teaching." (from *A Death in the Desert* by Robert Browning.)

Perhaps it helps not to think in terms of separating our triune being into body, mind and spirit, but to think of ourselves as one: a living soul. When we neglect our physical, mental or spiritual selves, we feel disjointed, frustrated, restless. But when we attend to each of our selves, there comes a unifying balance, an integration, a being one.

Running is good for my heart and lungs, my bones and muscles, and revs my metabolism. Running at long distances "clears the field"—empties the mind of anxious thoughts, of problems there seem no answer for, and obsessions; it unplugs a well of creative solutions and ideas. And then there is the "runner's high," a biochemical event during which endorphins—a sort of pain killer-mood elevator drug made by the body—are released.

I can tell when this is happening, about 40 minutes into my run. I feel energized and strong, as though I could run forever. I feel at one with the towering pines and whistling robins, the open sky and solid road, and with my self. Once I fell in love with an ancient, gnarled oak.

My morning run is often the only time of day I get out-of-doors. There's something about looking at walls.... Like the Bible story of Jacob's cows that looked at spotted poles and gave birth to spotted calves, my mind produces walls. Outdoors, I am recreated.

Running is often prayer and worship. Sometimes (when no one's looking) I run with my arms open wide, exuberant, free. In *Chariots of Fire*, Eric Liddle said, "When I run, I feel his pleasure."

There are always obstacles—some mental, some physical. I've had to stop running for months because of injuries from my own recklessness. If I push too hard—increase my mileage too quickly—my aging back rebels, not ready for the demands I place on it. If I do not replace my worn-down running shoes, the tendons in my high instep tear. If I get so caught up in the wonders of creation that I don't pay attention to the road, I'm likely to step in a pothole and sprain my ankle.

Sometimes I stop because of disruptions in my routine. Sometimes, I just don't feel like it.

When I stop running, I get heavy: overweight, sluggish, dull-witted, irritable. It is hard to get started again.

With all its benefits, running is not everything. If I neglect the writer, the lover, the mother, the pupil, the friend, the woman, the daughter of God, I become less than whole. I've clutched, at times, when the rest of my world has fallen apart, to running. It cannot carry the whole load. But it can keep me struggling forward. One foot in front of the other. To the next telephone pole, to the next mailbox, to the end of the road. It is not everything, but it is something.

I ran today.

Stripping Women of Dignity

It was so humiliating.

The guy at the counter spoke to me in a perfectly normal way, but the poster on the wall behind him screamed. It was a photo of four naked women, displaying their buttocks.

It was me, my daughters and my mother. It was the friendly woman at the grocery checkout; it was the cafeteria lady who serves my grandson his lunch; it was my best friends.

It was all of us and what it screamed was, "You are nothing! There is nothing special about you! You are worthless!"

As I stood there I felt embarrassed, ashamed to be a woman. I stood naked before this stranger. I wanted to pull a blanket around me from neck to toes.

Perhaps, under the facade of this make believe masculinity, that is the intention. Perhaps at one time in his life this man was emasculated by a woman. Perhaps his mother criticized everything he did or told him he was stupid or screamed at him a lot. So now he gets back at women by stripping them of their worth. Perhaps.

When I was in elementary school and had to present one of those dreaded oral reports, I was nervous about speaking in front of the class. My mother was the first to suggest the psychological tactic: "Just imagine they're all sitting there in their underwear."

Why? It put my classmates in a humiliating role and me in control.

I try to think of a parallel experience for men. What would make a man feel the shame and humiliation I did? What makes a man want to crawl away and hide and angry enough to fight, all at the same time?

I can only go by what I've observed. Men get angry enough to fight when their self-respect or manhood is challenged. Like being called "chicken," or criticizing their hot rod or motorcycle, or taunting their lack of strength or intelligence.

But beneath the anger lies something else. This quote from *The Chill* by Ross McDonald gives me a glimpse beneath the surface: "Black grief kept flooding up in him, changing to anger when it reached the air."

I am enraged when into my face is displayed an image of a stripped woman (me, my daughters, my mother). I want to smack the crap out of the man who owns the store. I want to shake the women who work there and say, "This is not OK. You've been lied to. You're better than this."

I tell my female friends about it. I tell them about the posters on the wall of the men's room at that store, about the stack of pornographic magazines in the corner. Your husbands and boyfriends, fathers and grandfathers, sons and grandsons go into that room and come out. Just thought I'd let you know.

For women and men who are free of inferiority complexes, it is a demeaning place to shop. Let's take our business elsewhere.

I wonder what it is about motorcycles and cars and other hobbies and sports that makes men want to strip women of their worth. I mean, you don't find scantily-clad women in pornographic poses in golf, bicycling or running magazines.

Though the women who participate in these sports may wear tight spandex outfits, their images are not pornographic. Their photos do not say "Come, buy me." The Greek word *porn* means prostitute.

Maybe that's because women have participated in those sports for so long. Magazine publishers know better than to market demeaning images to them, thereby turning away a large group of consumers.

Men who are secure in their masculinity respect women. They have no neediness driving them to see women "sitting there in their underwear."

I have no respect for men who must strip women. In spite of their football uniforms, their leather jackets, their muscle shirts, they are weak and needy, perhaps even abusive to the women in their lives.

The images on the posters, in the magazines, movies and websites, are not just anonymous generic immoral women whose souls do not matter to God.

It is you, your daughters and your mother.

Starving for Beauty

A lady never goes out without wearing a girdle, Mom always said.

Back in those days, in the 1950s, that meant stuffing the female proportions into a tiny perforated rubber sheath in order to bring it under control.

"See," my mother pointed once to a woman walking ahead of us. "That woman is not wearing a girdle. See how her rear end is jiggling?"

Unruly thing, the female body.

At the Museum of Modern Art in New York is an exhibit called "Extreme Beauty: The Body Transformed," which I read about in a newspaper. The exhibit focuses on fashions that have transformed the female body into…whatever was popular at the time.

"Extreme beauty" is relative.

For instance, the museum features neck rings, once worn by Ndebele and Padoung people as a way to lengthen the neck, seen as a symbol of grace, strength and poise, the story says. Japanese clothing flattened the chest while European empire gowns pushed the bust up and out.

We all know how Chinese women were forced to bind their feet to prevent them from growing. In the 16th century, Venetian women wore 20-inch high platform shoes (called *chopines*) to make them appear taller than the peasants. I can imagine all the sprained and broken ankles.

In the 19th century, undergarments began to be used to shape and reform the body. Bustles enhanced the hips while corsets cinched the waist, pushed up the bust and straightened the back. Breathing, I suppose, was secondary.

Today, a walk through a lingerie department shows how little progress we've made. Stretch elastic undergarments control the tummy and slim the thighs. Bra cups filled with foam, gel or water give a woman the appearance of having a large bust.

Many women today opt for cosmetic surgery and liposuction. Hips may no longer be in style, but lips are. Suck it off the hips, put it in the lips. For a few thousand bucks women can get big ones with collagen injections.

Seems rather primitive, doesn't it?

Diet and exercise also help reshape the body. In search of the perfect non-jiggly body, many young women today are starving and under-nourishing themselves.

Unfortunately, the search for perfection does not aim for character development. Our culture's female icons—yes, even after 9-11—do not encourage young women to seek the virtues of honesty, morality and charity. Role models—supermodels, pop music and TV stars—flaunt their self-seeking, immoral lifestyles while leaving young women craving the (current idea of a) perfect body. Today that means being skinny.

As a result, many young women are afflicted with anorexia and bulimia. Statistics show more of us Americans are overweight, but it seems too many are underweight as well. When I see the bony frames of young women on campus or in stores or at church, I automatically picture them throwing up in a toilet, or eating a green pea and Saltine cracker for dinner.

Donna Lou Shickel told me that when she worked as model in Hollywood, some 20 years ago, the other girls kept fainting during the workday for lack of food.

"It's a horrible business," she says.

If they do not kill themselves, in a few short years these young women will pay for blind foolishness. Their tampered-with metabolisms will be nearly incapable of burning calories, thereby turning unconsumed energy into fat. Not to mention always being cold.

When I think about the women I love and admire, I don't think about skinniness as a virtue. Women don't make a difference in the world by being skinny.

Mom, of course, was my biggest influence. And her girdle was part of the package of who she was. But I didn't think about that when she was reading me stories, playing catch with me or caressing my cheek. She was beautiful just the way she was.

Through Darkness Up to God

○ ○

"The most beautiful thing we can experience is the mysterious."

—*Albert Einstein*

Big Truth and little truth

Poems are made by fools like me
But only God can make a tree.

—Joyce Kilmer

"What would you say to the churches in Harrisonburg?" The question was posed to me as a journalist who writes about religion in the city.

I was embarrassed almost, to be asked such a question. As if my opinion mattered. But it does matter, as much and no more or less than anyone else's.

I offer observations. Not the voice of God. Not "Thus saith the Lord." Not "Jesus would say..." Just me, doodling.

I am not a theologian and so my observations are simplistic. Perhaps overly so.

The Truth around which Christianity has grown and continues to thrive is Jesus Christ. That is, God, out of his great love for man, coming to earth as a man, living his life among men, suffering and dying in punishment for our failings, rising from death three days later and, after that, ascending to his Father, thereby giving man the hope of living forever. (When I say 'man' or 'men,' I mean men and women, my understanding being that 'woman' means 'man with a womb.' I don't have a problem with that.)

Big Truth is also the two commandments Jesus gave, according to the New Testament, to "love the Lord your God with all your heart, with all your mind, with all your soul and with all your strength, and to love your neighbor as yourself."

Big Truth is the 10 Commandments.

Stuff like that.

How we live the big T stuff out, that's what makes little truth: traditions, rituals, individual callings, personal convictions. These little t's are important, too, but not central to our faith.

It is important for churches and Christians not to represent the little t (subjective) truth as Big T (objective) Truth. By this I mean that we should first and foremost learn and teach others to be followers of Christ.

"Until we know God, we seek to obey Him by doing things He neither commands nor cares about; while the things for which He sent His Son, we regard of little or no importance," said George MacDonald.

When I was growing up it seemed like my Catholic friends were being trained to be good Catholics. The tenets and traditions of the Roman Catholic Church were the focus of their faith. I have observed some of that among my Mennonite neighbors—and folks of many faiths—here in the valley. Well and good. Kids and new Christians need an identity, a people and tradition with which to identify, and particular disciplines when learning to follow Christ. Even "nondenominational" churches do this.

But when the little t's, the ways and means, are equated with big T, then you have pretty much written Jesus out of the picture. He becomes a figurehead, and the focus shifts to man's efforts to get cleaned up for God or close to God or to serve God. And these are much of what Christians fight about.

"What a pity that so hard on the heels of Christ come the Christians," wrote Annie Dillard.

First Communion was an important step in the religious life of my Catholic friends. Little girls wore frilly white dresses with white gloves, got a small white Bible and rosary beads. There was usually a party for the child and gifts, money.

Holy Communion is a big T, a sacrament commanded by Jesus. The bread and the wine are his body and blood. However, it was the pretty white dress, gloves, Bible and rosary beads and the party and gifts that my friends looked forward to and talked about afterwards.

The big T got lost in all the little t's.

I was once in a Sunday morning service where the pastor asked how individuals experienced the presence of the Holy Spirit. The answers came: shouting, dancing, laughing, singing, shaking. Nobody said "silence." That's somebody else's little t.

It's kind of like cooking. We all need protein to survive. Let's say beef. Eating it is vital. That we cook it is important. How we cook it is not. In Italy, it might be a meatball, in Mexico, an enchilada, in Germany, schnitzel, in Virginia, barbecue.

A close-minded and ignorant person would believe that barbecuing is the only way to cook beef, or even the best way.

A Mennonite acquaintance recently lamented that his sister was a Pentecostal. He felt she was missing so much of the Mennonite convictions on social justice. I imagine she feels her brother is missing the rich emotional element she experiences in worship. She tasted the enchilada and decided she liked her beef a little spicy.

What makes a good Catholic or Mennonite or Pentecostal is one's devotion to the dogmas and doctrines of their denomination. What makes a good Christian is one's faith in Jesus Christ, loving him with all their heart, soul and strength, and loving their neighbors as themselves.

That's what I have to say.

Covering God

It's been over a year since I began the "God beat" for the newspaper.

The word "religion" conjures very different images for different people. To some it means saintliness, to others it's loaded with judgement and condemnation, to some it means good works and to others it means just to believe.

The word gives me the creeps, because I equate it with "pious" or "sanctimonious." To be called religious feels like an insult, and I must remind myself that it depends on who's saying it. I think about that as I paste the section header—Religion—on the page each Friday.

As a child, I went to church four or five times—with my Dad to a Methodist church and with my Catholic cousin to Mass one Easter. My friends were Catholic and Jewish. I was fascinated with the hardware of their religions—rosary beads and yarmulkes and such—and how they got out of school at Yom Kippur and Ash Wednesday. If any of my friends were Protestant I am not aware of it: they never brought it up.

Mom began going to religious meetings when I was five or six. That's when the fights started between her and Dad. When he forbade her from going to the meetings, she went secretly, lying to him about where she'd been.

My neighborhood playmate, Lisa, told me that because I pronounced Hawaii as "Ha-va-he" I was making fun of God's creation, and that he would send me to hell for that.

Mom and Lisa were religious. When I began my search for God, I knew where not to look. If this Being was good and loving, then he had nothing to do with the fights. If he truly created all things and "whose dwelling is the light of setting suns, and the round ocean and the living air, and the blue sky and in the mind of man"—then he would not concern himself with petty rules.

Religion did that. Somehow, even quite young, I was able to separate people's ideas about God from who God might actually be.

"As I read the Old and New Testaments, I am struck by the awareness therein of our lives being connected with cosmic powers, angels and archangels, heavenly principalities and powers, and the groaning of creation. It's too radical, too uncontrolled for many of us, so we build churches, which are the safest possible places to escape God. We pin him down, far more painfully than he was nailed to the cross, so that he is rational and comprehensible and like us, and even more unreal"(Madeleine L'Engle).

Though I've always had an aversion to "organized religion," I've met many individuals within those organizations in whom I have caught a sense of the divine.

I have sensed God in the peaceful spirits of monks and nuns at mountain monasteries, in the tearful eyes of a soul-winning Baptist pastor, in the raucous "hallelujahs" at Pentecostal revivals, in the love of a Lutheran pastor for the people in her care, in the ancient chants, candlelight and incense of Russian Orthodox believers, in the people's plea of "Lord have mercy" at a Catholic funeral, in the determination of a Jewish rabbi to preserve and pass on the history and traditions of "God's chosen," in the strong convictions of an Orthodox Presbyterian minister.

After covering religion all this time, I am more aware than ever that, in spite of what we claim to know, none of us has all the answers. And that, if we worship "in spirit and in truth," it doesn't matter what form that worship takes—whether it's through carefully chosen hymns, folksy guitar music or big-band contemporary.

My most meaningful worship happens when I'm out walking, running, hiking, cycling. As we sang "O Come, O Come, Emmanuel," at church Sunday, I was struck by the line, "...And ransom captive Israel, That mourns in lonely exile here..." I felt my loneliness and thought of how lonely we all are.

I mean, when you get right down to it, we each must experience God to a depth that we cannot share with another human being, to a depth that has nothing whatsoever to do with anything we do at our place of worship.

Yet, as Gerald May writes in *Will and Spirit*, "even in our aloneness we are together, for we each have it. At the deepest levels of our hearts we are all aching, for each other and for the same eternally loving One who calls us. It would be well, I think, if we could acknowledge this more often to one another"—no matter what religion we are.

Encounter with the Cross in a Junk Shop

"Christ's cross is Christ's way to Christ's crown," advises William Penn in the preface to his book, *No Cross, No Crown*.

He began writing the "discourse," as he calls it, while imprisoned in the Tower of London in 1668, for publishing a brochure, *The Sandy Foundation Shaken*, in which he refuted the Calvinists.

I found *No Cross, No Crown*—it is undated though at least a hundred years old—at a Front Street junk shop in Shenandoah. Intrigued by the title, I paid the sticker price of 15 cents.

Get a load of the title page:

> *No Cross, No Crown.*
> *A discourse,*
> *showing the nature and discipline of*
> *The Holy Cross of Christ:*
> *and that the denial of self, and daily bearing of Christ's cross,*
> *is the alone way to the rest and kingdom of God.*
> *To which are added,*
> *the living and dying testimonies of many persons of fame and learning,*
> *both of ancient and modern times, in favour of this treatise.*
> *In Two Parts.*
>
> *—By William Penn.*

> *"And Jesus said to his disciples: If any man will come after me, let him deny*
> *himself, and take up his cross daily, and follow me. Luke iv. 23.—I have*
> *fought the good fight, I have finished my course, I have kept the faith:*
> *Henceforth there is laid up for me a crown of righteousness,*
> *&c. 2 Tim. iv. 7."*

Not a popular message today, not at all a message.

At the time I found this book, I was questioning many of the teachings of modern Christianity. Just the title seemed to be the uncovering of an ancient secret.

Penn writes: "The great work and business of the cross of Christ in man, is self-denial;…"

We do not hear about self denial in today's American churches. Many of the behaviors and practices we accept in today's church are a result of the natural resistance to death to self. In America, the church has been absorbed into the culture, and believers are promised the American Dream for their faithfulness.

Perhaps it is the church's alignment with the "ways of the world" that is causing attendance to drop, according to Barna Research. Why get up early Sunday for a church service that resembles a motivational seminar or a support group meeting or a consciousness-raising session?

Penn, an intimate co-worker with Friends founder George Fox, wrote that the knowledge of and obedience to the doctrine of the cross of Christ was the door to true Christianity. He contended that "unmortified Christians" and heathen bowed to the same god, the "lord of lusts," and occupied their time and conversation with the same subjects:

"What shall we eat? What shall we drink? What shall we wear? And how shall we pass away our time? Which way may we gather wealth, increase our power, increase our territories…?"

Penn observes that the great conquerors of history, Caesar and Alexander, "vanquished others, not themselves," whereas Christ conquered self. Penn knew what he was talking about.

He was the son of Admiral William Penn, a highly respected and rich military commander in England. When Penn did not remove his hat—a sign of respect—in the presence of the king, his father became quite angry, demanding that he do so. The Quakers believe no one human being deserves any more respect than another.

Rather than justify the use of his father's name and money to further the kingdom of heaven, Penn followed his conscience, and was subsequently kicked out of his father's house and threatened with being disinherited. As we well know, in spite of his choice, Penn did not die in obscurity.

In looking to Christ as our example, we've skipped the cross and gone right on to the crown. In America, that means we look good with our gym-toned bodies and current fashions, we feel good because our self-esteem has been pumped up with seminars and popular books, and we do good, giving to "those less fortunate" at all the appropriate holidays and times of disaster.

We do not lay our pride, our arrogance, our self-sufficiency or our ambition at the cross, because we need them to achieve and maintain and progress in glory. We "Christianize" our traits, talents and assets.

The second part of *No Cross, No Crown*, Penn illustrates his point with the testimonies of people throughout history, including Socrates, Plato and Aristotle, Sir Walter Raleigh, Princess Elizabeth of the Rhine and his own father.

Penn's father came to respect his son greatly and, shortly before he died, charged his son with three things, the first of which he learned from his son: "Let nothing in this world tempt you to wrong your conscience."

Sentimental Journey

I spent the spring digging around in the past, the religious past of the Shenandoah Valley.

After reading of the early settlers to the Valley—braving Indian raids, breaking their backs to clear land for gardens and houses and cattle, leaving home, going where they did not know in order to live by their consciences—I found myself idealizing their courage and faith.

And I wonder, as the wilderness was tamed and the settlers aged, if they too became tame, complacent, with only their memories to remind them of the adventures they lived walking hand in hand with God.

For a people or a person who can point to a collective or personal past in which God has been real and faithful and miracle-working it is easy later, once life has settled down, to have a backward-looking religion. Based on a miraculous experience or revelation or blessed time period that is gone.

A sentimental faith.

Sentimental faith dwells on what God did yesterday. I weep sometimes at God's mercy, how he forgave my crimes against him and me and those I love and against strangers and enemies. And I long for yesterday, when I had many troubles but they seemed so far away because he was so present.

When our faith is of the sentimental sort, we pray on yesterday's faith (to use musician Ben Arthur's turn of phrase), but without yesterday's results.

Yesterday's faith was for yesterday's challenges. When my faith is based on yesterday or last year or last decade, I am ill-prepared for today. Though it may seem a paradox, God often seems nearer in the midst of hardship and tragedy than in times of prosperity and complacency.

Perhaps it is my subconscious trying to keep me from dealing with the more serious issues that surface as I "mature." The issues that confront me today, from without and within, I cannot stand up to with yesterday's youthful faith.

Recalling the miracles of the past, the things he's brought me through, is futile unless the memories stimulate my faith in God for today's demands.

God made this clear to the Israelites when they wandered through the wilderness after their sensational exit from Egypt. He gave them fresh food every day, called it manna. The Israelites were to gather it from the ground each morning. If they stored some for the next day, it rotted. They had to depend on God to be "I am" every day.

God provided the manna yesterday and the day before that. That should have helped them believe he would do it again today. I must gather it afresh each day.

In a larger sense, denominations, ministries and spiritual movements often operate on yesterday's faith, losing their relevance as the world changes or as the adherents mature in their faith.

We see this in the many churches attended by only the elderly. The church and its members point back with a sentimental feeling to a time when it all meant so much. So let's keep doing it that way.

We see this when people face difficulties that their church is not equipped to help them with. Many denominations were founded on a revelation that over time becomes theologically and in practice overdeveloped, while other truths are ignored. In this case, sentimentality fosters an obsessive devotion to the founders, long dead, and their precepts.

God is not a yesterday kind of guy. He is not an old man. He is always now, forever.

Sentimental faith is often accompanied by someday faith.

When we hear his voice today, telling us to apologize to our spouse, to send $20 to a distant friend, to tell the truth and so risk losing our jobs, to quit work to raise our children, to trust him with overwhelming emotions rather than smoking or drinking—but we dismiss it or put it off or flat out refuse, then we risk losing the ability to hear him the next time.

We think, "Tomorrow I will be stronger in my faith" or "It can wait" or "God understands I can't do it because of my weakness."

Because we don't want to hear him. Not really.

Today is the day.

When Moses asked God what his name was, God did not reply, "I was" or "I will be" or even "I should be" or "I could be." He said, "I am."

And we are too.

Speak, Lord

Who speaks for God?

The seminar title caught my attention. The teacher, Jim Wallis, is editor of Sojourner magazine. While I cannot say for sure how Wallis intended to answer that question, I do have a letter from him in which he once and for all informs us who does not speak for God.

You've got The Right and you've got The Left. And then there's Jesus. And you've got people taking the name of Jesus and saying, "Thus saith the Lord," or "If Jesus were here today he would..." You've got groups like The Community and Jehovah's Witnesses claiming to be the true Israel, God's elect. You've got "prophets" like Sun Yung Moon claiming to be the present incarnation of Christ. You've got J.Z. Knight channeling the ancient Ramtha, claiming to help us find God in ourselves.

To whom do we listen? Who does speak for God?

In her last week's Santa Barbara News-Press column, "What Would Jesus Do?," Diana Butler Bass makes some all-knowing statements on that subject: Jesus would vote Socialist. Jesus would oppose the military-industrial complex. Jesus would condemn tobacco companies. Jesus would not be caught dead at a Promise Keepers rally.

Wow, it seems like Jesus feels the same as Bass on all those issues. It's no wonder atheists claim that believers have created God in their image.

As religion editor, I get mail from lots of religious groups. Groups that make absolute statements on these and many other issues, claiming to represent the opinions of God.

Bass has a Ph.D., so perhaps she is privy to information about Jesus that I'm not. The only way I can tell about What Would Jesus Do is by What Jesus Did when he was here. If Bass is basing her beliefs about Christ on what we know of him in the Bible, I find it difficult to know how she reached her conclusions:

As for voting Socialist, Jesus did share what he had: multiplying the loaves and fishes, healing the sick, turned the water into wine...but he did not petition or command the Roman government or the Jewish leaders to do so.

In reality, Jesus did not oppose the military-industrial complex of his day. He said little about the Roman military. He did, though, raise from the dead the daughter of a Roman officer.

As for condemnation, the only scathing words Jesus had for anyone in the New Testament was to religious leaders: the blind leading the blind, to those who presumed to speak for God.

As for showing up at the meetings of the patriarchal oppressors—as Bass and other who are afraid of the Promise Keepers claim them to be—Jesus showed up just about anywhere he thought someone might listen to him, from the synagogue to the drinking parties.

I have learned much from Bass's past columns. I have heard the voice of God through her, have clipped her columns about Easter and women and the desert experience. I will continue to read and learn from her, but I'd be an idiot to think that her pen is permanently dipped in a special inkwell of God's anointing.

Paul, the ultimate patriarchal oppressor, had his hang-ups, too. But in spite of his history-changing revelations about who Christ was and what Christ did for mankind, he was not presumptuous enough to think every little thought he had came from the mind of God. He wrote things like, "Follow me as I follow Christ" and "It is I who say this, not the Lord."

Let's face it, a lot of folks are taking the Lord's name in vain, trying to manipulate us with Scripture. A typical "panic letter" from a religious or political group will start out with a quote or an example of something done by the Left or Right. This is to show how horrible they are. Then they'll describe how wonderful we are. How we, this scraggly remnant, are standing for God's will. If only we had more money…

Um, I don't think so.

The Religious Left claims the Religious Right is taking over the country, legislating morality, while the Right says the Left is taking over the country, legislating caring.

From what I see in the Bible, and in spite of being Lord of the universe, Jesus wasn't really a legislative kind of guy. He related to people one on one: touching, holding, healing, discussing, teaching, respecting.

Jesus said the way to heaven is narrow, not narrow-minded. It's much easier to cop out and let others—"experts"—tell us what God is saying than to do the work of growing up and learning to hear him for ourselves.

Because—surprise, surprise—God can and does speak for Himself.

Love My Enemies? Are You Kidding?

The signs this fall are everywhere:

"God bless America."

"Pray for the victims and their families."

"Pray for our leaders."

"God bless our troops."

These are natural admonitions. Easy to say, easy to do. We flock to church services to pray. We ask God to comfort, protect, give wisdom. Our first and continuing cry over the victims in the towers and Pentagon, the victims in the airplanes, the firefighters and police officers, is "Oh, God!"

What is difficult—extremely difficult—is this admonition Jesus Christ gave to his followers:

"You have heard that they were told, 'Love your neighbor and hate your enemy.' But what I tell you is this: Love your enemies and pray for your persecutors…" (Matt: 5:43–44)

Wow, Jesus. How can you say that? Are you crazy? Did you see what they did to us? Didn't you see the people on fire jumping out the windows of the World Trade Center? Don't you know about the firefighters who died trying to save people?

And that's not all. He goes on to say, "…only so can you be children of your heavenly Father." (Matt 5:45)

You mean if I don't love those terrorists I am not a child of God? That can't be in the Bible. It can't be.

It is. It is what makes Christianity different. It is what makes followers of Christ different than people like Osama Ben Ladin and Muhammed Atta and the Taliban. As a matter of fact, it is the only thing that distinguishes us.

"If you love only those who love you, what credit is that to you? Even sinners love those who love them. Again, if you do good only to those who do good to you, what credit is there in that? Even sinners do as much," Jesus said. (Luke 6:32-33)

Loving our enemies has the power to transform us to be like God. To form us into a whole different sort of human being than our enemies.

This does not mean we excuse what they did. It does not mean we feel affection or fondness for them. It does not mean trying to think they are really not that bad, because they really are that bad.

C.S. Lewis struggled with this and came to think of it this way: "In my most clear-sighted moments not only do I not think myself a nice man, but I know that I am a very nasty one."

In looking at his enemies, Lewis writes, he remembered being taught to "love the sinner, hate the sin," and wondered how he could hate the sin without hating the man.

"But years later it occurred to me that there was one man to whom I had been doing this all my life—namely myself. However much I might dislike my own cowardice or conceit or greed, I went on loving myself," Lewis writes. "…Just because I loved myself, I was sorry to find I was the sort of man who did those things."

I may not be capable of killing 5,000 people with a jumbo jet, but I am capable of some really cruddy crappy things. Things I am ashamed to speak of. Things I do not like to admit. Things I hate.

And, as Lewis says, Jesus does not require us to reduce the hatred we feel for such cruel and inhuman acts. We are to hate them, "in the same way in which we hate things in ourselves: being sorry that the man should have done such things, and hoping, if it is any way possible, that somehow, sometime, somewhere, he can be cured and made human again."

Last night I found this prayer.

O Lord, remember not only the men and women of good will, but also those of ill will. But do not remember all the suffering they have inflicted on us; remember the fruits we have bought, thanks to this suffering—our comradeship, our loyalty, our humility, our courage, our generosity, the greatness of heart which has grown out of all this, and when they come to judgement let all the fruits which we have borne be their forgiveness.

(Prayer written by an unknown prisoner in Ravensbruck concentration camp and left by the body of a dead child.)

Look at some good things, the fruits that have come from the horrible events of Sept. 11.

We have discovered our true heroes are the firefighters and rescue workers who live next door, not drug-snorting, bed-hopping celebrities. We have discovered we can pray with our Jewish, Catholic, Protestant and Muslim neighbors. We have discovered our reason for living is not to get more stuff than our neighbors, but to love and get to know our neighbors. We have discovered we are capable of giving our hard-earned cash to someone who needs it more than we do.

And on and on.

Christians have the opportunity to be transformed. God did not cause this horror: it is the work of evil incarnate. And God's plan, always at work beneath the surface of human events, is redemption, always to transform evil into good. That's what he did on the cross. That is the message of the cross.

Let's not blow it.

Love My Enemies? (Part II)

My dad was a veteran of the Korean war.

He was a cook. He used to show a picture of him leaning in the doorway of the mess hall kitchen, wearing a large white apron and cotton cap.

I asked him if he was ever in combat. He always evaded answering that question, but he did say he hated "gooks." His bitterness gave me the impression that he may have witnessed some atrocious acts that he wished not to recall.

My mother said when she was pregnant with me, she wanted to name me "Kim," but my dad refused because it was a popular Korean name. And he hated Koreans.

I wish he could have talked about it to someone, gotten rid of the hatred.

It is unfortunate that war begins in defense of principles or people and ends in bitter hatred. Hatred is no motivator. After the war is over, what have you got? A bunch of people who have been destroyed within by hatred.

This is what I was talking about in a column I wrote a few weeks ago about Jesus' admonition to love our enemies. And I began to wonder if it was possible to engage in war with an enemy while loving him.

I remembered the scene in *Star Wars* movie, *Return of the Jedi*, in which Luke Skywalker is engaged in battle with Darth Vader. Vader is an evil warrior whose leader and mentor is the Emperor. In an earlier movie, Luke discovers that Vader is his father and that he had been a noble Jedi knight until the Emperor turned him to the dark side.

In this movie, Luke discovers that he has a twin sister, too—Princess Leia. He cares deeply for Leia.

Though common sense and his friends tell him otherwise, Luke loves his father and feels Vader can be turned back to the good side.

In one of the movie's final scenes, the Emperor tries to turn Luke, a Jedi knight, to the dark side. He forces a confrontation between father and son, Vader and Skywalker. Vader persistently attacks Luke with his light saber. The Emperor looks on, goading Luke to "feel the hate, kill your father."

The fight scene moves from level to level as father and son become exhausted. Luke tries to talk his father into defecting from the evil side, seemingly to no avail. "I can feel the good in you," he tells Vader.

This impasse continues until, during a pause, Vader picks up on Luke's thoughts about his sister, who Vader did not know existed. Vader says "...a twin sister? Your feelings betray you. If you will not turn to the dark side, perhaps she will."

Luke screams "Nooooooo!" and begins fighting with a purpose: to prevent Vader from hurting Leia.

His love for his sister motivates him to fight. Though he loves his father, too, he wounds him. Then the Emperor steps in to finish Luke off. If Luke will not come to the dark side, then he must die. The Emperor tortures Luke with pain while Vader watches. Then, when Luke is writhing in agony, Vader turns and picks up the Emperor and throws him into a deep chasm.

As Vader is dying, Luke comforts him. Father and son look into each other's eyes. Vader's face is full of love for his son. He dies in peace.

Star Wars is a modern-day fairy tale. Like the ones I used to tell my children that always had "the moral of the story."

In the end, Luke proved to be, not a peacekeeper, but a peacemaker. Had he been motivated by hate to kill Vader, his father would have been forever lost to him. The conflict was going to happen no matter what, but it was love that made all the difference in the outcome.

The Lord Giveth.

"The Lord giveth, and the Lord taketh away," a tearful Russell Yates said at the June 27 funeral of his five children. The Houston man's wife had drowned the children in the couple's bathtub.

Did the Lord taketh away the Yates children? Did God bless Russell Yates with five children and then change his mind and take them away?

We say that God is good, full of mercy and grace. Is it good to kill young children?

We say the Bible is "God's Word." But do we care to understand, or do we just pull out random verses to support our feelings?

Let's take off our religion caps and use a teensy weensy bit of our everyday common sense here.

"The Lord giveth, and the Lord taketh away" is a quote from the mouth of Job. Job was not a prophet speaking for God. He was also—like Russell Yates—a father who lost all his children—seven sons and three daughters—in a few minutes time.

When he was told his children had all been killed, Job's reaction was to worship God. The full quote of what he said is, "Naked came I from my mother's womb, and naked shall I return; the Lord gave, and the Lord has taken away; blessed be the name of the Lord."

Job was telling God that no matter what happened, he would continue to trust him. As for his attributing God with the taking of his children, Job was speaking in ignorance. Yes, Job is "blameless and upright." He "fears God and turns away from evil." But he does not know everything. By the end of the Book of Job—and it takes 42 chapters to accomplish this—Job realizes how ignorant he is about who God really is.

In the first few paragraphs of the Book of Job, it says Satan came to present himself before God and, during the course of their conversation about Job, Satan dared God to let him have Job for awhile. "So Satan went forth from the presence of the Lord" to do wicked things to Job.

So often we hear and read, when people die, things like, "God took him" or "God saw fit to take him." Actually, in the Bible, the only person it says God took was Elijah. And God did it like this: "And as they till went on and talked, behold, a chariot of fire and horses of fire separated the two of them. And Elijah went up by a whirlwind into heaven." (2 Kings 2:11)

That's a little different than drowning kids in a bathtub, seeing someone decline with disease or get killed in a car wreck.

God did not invent death. When he created the earth, the trees and plants, the fish, birds and animals, and then man, he saw that it was good. When Adam disobeyed God by eating the fruit, thereby bringing death into the world, God did not say that was good. As a matter of fact, God must have been bummed. Here, out of his goodness, he created all this life and beauty and now it all was doomed to die.

God is good. The word "good" does not evoke images of disease and death. It evokes smiles and flowers and kindness, life and happiness. Good parents do not punish their children by inflicting them with illness or by killing them. Neither does God.

In the last chapter of Job, after God has it out with Job, Job repents of his ignorance. He says, "But I have spoken of things which I have not understood, things too wonderful for me to know…I knew of you then only by report, but now I see you with my own eyes."

"…Thus the Lord blessed the end of Job's life more than the beginning…"

The Lord giveth. Period.

Love Should be the Referee Of the Scripture Wars

If I have the gift of prophecy and can fathom all mysteries and all knowledge, and if I have a faith that can move mountains, but have not love, I am nothing.

—1 Corinthians 13:2.

I see the Scripture Wars are still being waged on the editorial page and the radio.

This is where a few of the religious folks in these parts get to tell the rest of us not only how to live but how to think. The correct way. Their way. Using the Holy Bible as a weapon.

Seven or eight years ago there was an argument running on the editorial page over whether Abraham Lincoln was a Christian. One person pointed to the prayers of the former president, the references to God in his speeches and to his moral convictions.

The opposing side argued that Mr. Lincoln could not have been a Christian because he was not a member of any church.

My concern was not with Mr. Lincoln's religious status but with the premise that membership in a church signified whether one was or was not a Christian. Unfortunately, I set my opinion on paper and sent it to the editorial page.

Church membership, I wrote, while it may be advantageous in many ways, is irrelevant to the question of Mr. Lincoln's Christianity.

I say unfortunately because the most high reverend something or other, who was involved in the war of words over Mr. Lincoln, phoned to set me straight on just how vital church membership was to one's salvation. While the Rev. may have had loyal followers who said "amen" to his every word, I did not become one of them that morning.

Last week, however, I changed a political opinion I'd held for many years. Not because someone derided me for how wrong I was, nor from watching a manipulative movie or TV show. Certainly not by being attacked with scriptures. But by inquiring, by listening, by thinking, by listening, by reading.

Changing my opinion about the issue was liberating. My former opinion was not something I'd ever given any thought to, but had absorbed from the people I hung around with. Kind of like wearing a dress your mother likes on you, even though the color is all wrong for your complexion, and the length is unflattering to your particular figure.

My revised opinion feels terrific on me.

Ever have a friend you love to argue with? Someone you can express your opinion to freely, knowing you'll still be friends after? Someone who does not demean you in any way or smear your motives and character? If so you are blessed.

One such friend of mine is politically and spiritually the opposite of me. He challenges me to explain my position—making me think and give voice to why I believe what I do. And while most of his arguments have not changed my mind about the issues over which we disagree, I have learned a lot by listening to him.

I have seen my views through his eyes.

The Scripture Wars remind me of the Inquisition, the aim of which was to "save the heretic's soul," thus purging the land of evil forces. Although I'm not sure what is the point of the present battle. There seems to be no pretense at saving souls, but at parading a perverse sort of superiority.

I turn the radio off. Because of the questionable motives and know-it-all attitudes, I can't even listen to the speakers I agree with. I feel kind of sorry for them, like they've missed the point.

"Love is patient, love is kind. It does not envy, it does not boast, it is not proud. It is not rude, it is not self-seeking, it is not easily angered, it keeps no record of wrongs. Love does not delight in evil but rejoices with the truth…"

If it ain't loving, it ain't God. That doesn't mean we can't express our views forcefully or passionately. But so much being debated in the name of God is just so peripheral. I mean, what does it matter whether a person is baptized as a child or as an adult? Or if they're baptized three times forward or one time back?

Do they love God and their fellow humans—Catholic, Protestant, humanist, conservative, liberal?

God is love. That is all. God is love.

0-595-25802-6